Of the birth of S. Clare and of the etimologie of the names of the mother and the daughter.

CHAP, VII,

Notwithstanding that for the moſt part names are impoſed accidentaly and are giuen to children according to the will and pleaſure of their parents yet many times it falleth out that the conditions of the perſon doth agree with the denominatiõ , & this wee find in holy writ, B. *Hortulana*, and glorious S. *Clare* may ſerue vs for an inſtance; for *Hortulana* in our tongue may be called Gardiner and not without great miſterie conſidering ſhe was to produce ſo noble & virtuous a plant in the garden of the holy Church, which hath taken ſuch encreaſe that her bowes and branches haue ſpread and extended ouer all the corners of the world ſo that the birdes of heauen haue harboured and built their neſts in the bowes therof, that is a number of Religious ſoules who ſoaring vp with the wings of virtues doe raiſe vp them ſelues from terreſtriall things ,fixing their thoughts on the contemplation of Celeſtiall things, ſitting on the bowes of this tree to enioy the ſhade & ſhelter therof, there they remaine in heart and affection according

The etimologie of the name of Hortulana

The birds of heauen are the religious of ſainte Clare.

M 3 to

to the saying of the diuine Apostle, *our con-*
seruation is in heauen: these virgins hauing an
essay of the pleasant sweetnes of this plât grafted by the wise & prudent gardener *Hortulana:*
haue made more reckoning of their poore and
contemptible habit, of a straight and narrow
Cell, of base and humble offices, of a slender
and vnsauorie portion, taking more content
therin, then the Ladies oft! is world doe find
in their curious and fine dressings, their high
and honorable titles, their stately and magnificent Pallaces, and their dantie delicious dishes.
Now if the name of the mother hath giuen vs
subiect and matter to discourse of a garden, the
name of the daughter will serue for a warrent
& guide to ope the doore to all such as desire
to enter into it, to take the sent of these odoriferous flowers and fruitfull plants: *B. Hortu-*
lana being great with child & knowing herselfe
to be neere her downe lyig prayig vnto God in
a Church before a *Crucifix* beseechig the diuine
maiestie to Free her from all perill of death
in her childbirth which she much apprehēded,
she heard a voice proceeding from the *Crucifix*
which sayd, *feare not woeman for without danger*
thou halt bring forth a light which shall illumina-
te the whole world: hauing receiued this cōsolation and aduise from the diuine Oracle & being
deliuered with great ioy the yeare 1194, she
caused the name of Clare to be giuen to the
child at her Baptisme beleeuing firmely that in
her should be accōplished whatsoeuer was or-

Phil: 5.

Chr. p. 1.
l. 3. c. 1.
Wadd.
ad ann.
1212.
§. 15.
the cru-
cifix
speakes
to B. Hor-
tulana

dayned

ned and fortold by the diuine goodnes, neither
was the hope she conceiued of the accompli-
shment of the promise made her by the heauē
ly Oracle made void, for she bestowed on the
world a great light, & on heauen a great Sainte
according to the straine sūg in her prayse, *Clara*
re, Clara nomine: for she hath bene a light illumi-
nating the Church not only by name or renowne but effectuail by the refulgent Rayes of
of her admirable works and heroyicall acts, &
her life adorned with the lustre of all virtues
hath worthyly produced a number of rare flowers who by (the fragrancie and sweet Odour
of their supereminent perfections) haue perfu-
med the whole world, and the most bright
Rayes of this now light haue penetrated in to
the Pallaces of Princesses and Duchesses, darting their splendor in to the secret Clossets of
Queenes and Empresses in such sort that many
Ladyes being sought in Marryage by Dukes
Kings, Emperous, and Monarkes haue refused
those Royall Espousalls together with all dignities, riches and delights, for to embrace
Pouertie Humility, Chastity, pennance and
mortification in imitation of this resplendant
light, the practise of Chastitie and the florishing garlandes of virginitie which were almost
withered and decayed, did now againe reuiue
in the world a new spring arising from the
heat and splédor of her life, adorning her beautifull garden with all sort of fragrant flowers
of virtues.

*Of the infancie of S. Clare and of
her virtuons exercises,*

CHAP. VIII.

*Chr p.1
i. 8 c .2.*

Lare the litle plant of B. Hortulana faire
like the day, and gratious like an Angell,
began presently to appeare and shine like
a morning starre or faire *Aurora*, after the darke
night of this world: for in her tender yeares
and first infancie she expressed many signes of
mature sanctity, wherby she manifested the
goodnes of her nature, and the fauor wherwith
God had indued her: she was of nature very
tender and delicate, and of Capacity very apt
and docile, she learned of her mother the first
groūdes of Catholicke Religiō: the holy Ghost
by little and little framing this pure vessell of
election till he brought it to the fullnes of di
uine grace and perfection: her greatest delight
and content was in piety and deuotion, in pray
er she seemed to speake to God & his Angels:
frequently withdrawing her selfe frō company
to powre forth her selfe in her Oratorie, there
she layd open her heart and affection to her
Creator powring forth riuers of sacred teares
from her eyes: it was a thing very remarkable
in this her tender yeares to see that not hauing
beades wheron to say her prayers she made vse
of a heape of little stones wherwith she num

*Wadd
ad anni
1212.
§ 17.
Niceph l
11, c. 36*

bred

bred both the Paters and Aues, in this fort she
fayd her deuotions in imitation of the deuout
Father *Paul* liuing on the mount of *Phermes*
who euery day fayd three hundred prayers hauing as many ftones in his lap , and euery time
cafting one to the ground he payd as it were a
tribute to God this little virgin beginning to
feele the firft feruours of diuine loue, iudged
she muft contemne all tranfitorie apparence &
painted flowers of this world , and being in
prayer well inftructed by the holy Ghoft she
refolued as a wife fpirituall merchant to haue
no more regard to terreftriall affaires acknowledging them vnworthy to be efteemed, she
did weare as an other *S. Cecily* a hairecloth
vnder her rich and coftly apparell fo exteriourly fatisfying the world, and interiourly
her God and Creatour,

*Chr. p. x.
l. 8, c. 2,*

She was wholy addicted to the works of
mercie, bearing a fingular affectió to the poore
and needy being not ignorant that he that có-
paffionateth the poore and diftreffed, compaf-
fionateth *Chrift Iefus*, in their perfon, and to
the end her facrifice might be more pleafing
vnto God the moft delicate meats that were
giuen her for the nourishment of her little
body, she hid and gaue it fecretly to the poore,
knowing by diuine light , that fecret Almes
are moft meritorious, it fuffifing to be feene by
him who can recompence the act, to auoid all
oftentation and vaine honour , for otherwife
the applaufe of the world might be the recó-

N pence

pence of the liberalitie, in this sort the soule
of little *Clare* was replenished with Charity
and compassion; But hauing attained to ripe
age she was perswaded by her Parents to
make choice of a husband: she amased at the
sound of such an Allarum remained wounded
in her heart at the noice of these vngratfull tidings (which to a pure virgin is a martirdome)
to which she would neuer consent, but sought
euasions and delayes therby protracting time
the best she could to shunne maryage still recommending her Chastity to *Christ Iesus* her
spouse with all the other virtues wherwith
her soule was inriched; making a generous resolution to dye rather then to permit the Lillie
of her virginall purity to be in the least sort
soiled or faded, wherfore by all her indeauours
she laboured to augment the lustre therof, and
to become more gratious in the eyes of her
Creator and heauenly spouse. Such were the
first fruits of her spirit and the tokens of her
sanctitie: so that being anoynted with such a
sweet and precious oyntment she yeelded a
most fragrant sauour as a closet replenished
with most delightfull liquors, whose per-
fumes though they be shut vp discouer and
manifest themselues, and in such sort this holy
Virgin began without her knowledge to be
extolled by her neighbours, the true fame of
her secret pious works so publishing theselues
that in an instant they were exceedingly spread
abroad and euery where diuulged.

How

How S. Clare *came to the know-ledge of* S, Francis.

CHAP, IX.

THis Celestiall Doue *Clare*, hearing the great fame of the admirable life of S. *Francis* who then renewed to the world the way of perfection in the same Citie, with a maruellous example of pietie and sanctitie, and considering that many Gentlemen did follow him and that his life was allready approued by our holy mother the Church she conceiued a great desire to see and heare him, & to disclose vnto him her generous resolutions, S. *Francis* zealous of the good of soules and hauing heard the fame of her virtue, wayted the oportunity to meet with her, with intention to frustrate the world of so noble and pretious a prey, to present her to our soueraigne Redeemer, to serue him in some notable enterprise as preordayned of God to giue the foile to the prince of darcknes; neither did his diuine maiesty faile to open vnto them both the meanes, inspiring this virtuons Damsell to rely vpon an honorable and graue ancient matrone called *Bonne Guelfuccij* who gouerned her in her house as her mother: and to the end that her holy purpose might not be sinisterly

Luc. *Wadd.* *ad annũ* 1112. §. 18,

inter-

interpreted and to hinder publick murmure,
she went forth with this good Matrone, vsing
such prudent diligéce that she found him whō
her soule desired, that she might receiue from
his mouth as from the secretarie of the holy
Ghost the diuine instructions of her saluation.
The holy Father hauing louingly entertained
her began to preach vnto her the contempt of
the world, and by euident reasons to demon-
strate vnto her that all the beauty of things present is but vanity filled with false and deceitfull
hopes: he intimated vnto her the shortnes of
this life and the continuance of eternitie, the
obstacles and impediments in the way of saluation, and the many perils and snares which
in the wide way of the world doe draw to
damnation, then he propounded to her chast
eares the honorable and amiable espousales of
Iesus Christ, perswading her to conserue the O-
rient pearle of her virginall purity for her
heauenly Spouse, who out of the loue he bare
to vs being God became man and would be
borne of a virgin. Thus the holy Father solicited that affaire, playing the part of a true Pa-
ranymph and Embassadour of the heauenly
King, these diuine words penetrated the soule
of this holy Damsell, her heart being set on fire
with diuine loue, she now beganne very exqui-
sitly to dispose her selfe to affect his pious exhortations, which she esteemed to be more
then humaine, the world became irksome
vnto her, desiring to dye vnto it, wherfore

begin-

beginning already to tast the sweetnes of heauenly contemplation she resolued to embrace a most innocent and holy life, she melted as it were with the loue of her heauenly spouse, after whom she thirsted with a languishing desire.

The holy resolution of Sainte Clare,

CHAP. X.

When I consider the Lyon of *Sampson* lying dead in the lād of the Philistins, the throat filled with hony and the bowells with cruelty; I deeme it to be the true type of the world, which hath many pleasures, Flatterie, and delights in apparance, but hath the bowells of a Lyon stuffed with cruelty, treacherie and deceit, it deceiueth a man and withdraweth him from the seruice of God, profereth him many comforts, pleasures and charming delights, it feineth friendship promising honours dignities and promotions: but all tendeth to mischiefe, leading to vtter ruine and distructiō yea to eternall damnation. The wise and prudent Damsell *Clare* well considering the vanity and deceit therof, made a holy resolution to set it at naught, despicing and trampling vnder foot all honours, dignities, mariages, suōtuous apparell, Iewells, and all wordly pelfe and to

*Iud.*14

ded *i.*

dedicate her selfe a liuing temple to *Chrisſt Ieſus*
taking him for the only ſpouſe of her body, and
hauieg wholy ſubmitted her ſelſe to the coun-
ſels of the Seraphicall Father, she went vnto
him with great feruour of ſpirit demanding of
him whē and in what ſort she ſnould make her
retire from the world; whervpon the holy
father S. *Francis* ordained that an Palme Sūday
she should come to the proceſſió with the reſt
of the people apparrelled in moſt rich & ſumptuous manner, and that the night following she
should goe forth of the City abandoning all the
world and change the ſecular pleaſures into lamentations of the death and paſſion of our ſacred Redeemer: vpon Palme Sunday this Innocent Doue came to the proceſſion of the
great Church in the company of her mother &
other Ladyes; where ſell out a paſſage worthy
to be recorded as being done by the diuine ordination which was that all the other Ladyes
going according to the cuſtome of *Italy*, to
take holy Palme and S. *Clare* with rare modeſty
out of a virginall baſhfullnes remained alone
without mouing out of her place; the Biſhop
deſcending from the ſteppes of his ſeate, put
into her hid a branch of Palme, a true preſage
and argument of what ſhould be fall to this cō-
ſtant damſell: for our B. Sauiour repreſented
by the Biſhop would inſinuate that the ſame
night she should aſcend to the Palme to gather the pleaſant fruiſt therof.

  The Palme is the ſimbole of patience and

con-

Luc.
Wadd.
ad annū
1212 §.
19 20.

Caut. 7.

conftance, for it doth not shrinck at any op-
preſſion but the more you goe about to depreſſe
and hold it downe by force or waight, the more it aſcends and ſpreads is branches aloft. In
like ſort this couragious ſeruant of God was
within ſhort time to be depreſſed & humbled
by her friendes & kindred, making tryall of all
their power and force to withdraw her from
her pious deſignes, but ſtill, the more ſhe ray-
ſed vp her ſelfe in conſtancie, ſo that in fine
they were conſtrained to depart yeelding
them ſelues vanquiſhed by her generoſitie.

The Palme is the ſigne of victory, the triũ-
phant hand of the Conqueror being euer honoured with a Palme, the ſecretarie of our Redeemer doth auouch that he receiued from
God the fauour to behold in heauen the ſoules of the Bleſſed clothed in white ſhining
garments, and Palmes in their hands to declare the victorie they had gained ouery the Diuell & his tẽptations. The Biſhop gaue this dã-
ſell the miſterious Palme to declare that ſhe
ſhould triumph ouer the Diuell, the world, and
the fleſh by her teares and pennances: The
Palme doth alwaỹs conſerue its greeneſſe and
amongſt all coulors there is not any that doth
more comfort and ſtrengthen the ſight then
greene, S. *Clare* receiued the Palme by the ordination of God frõ the hands of the Biſhop
for to ſignify that ſhe ſhould alwayes conſerue
the fleſh greene of her virginall purity, a virtue moſt gratious and pleaſing to the eyes of
the

The Palme is the ſimbole of victorie. Apoc. 5.

The Palme is the type of virginitie.

the diuine maiesty : making the person like vnto the Angells according to the testimonie of our B.Sauiour, seruing for a mirour to draw many damsells in imitation of her to dedicate the integrity of their virginall purity to their heauenly spouse.

The Palme brings forth plesant fruits.

The Palme hath moreouer this propertie that it produceth Dates, a fruict very pleasant and delicious though late, for first it must for many yeares be carefully cultiuated, and indure very much by the sharpnes and rigour of the winter, by snow, rayne, haile and tempests, euen so this incomparable Virgin was a long time (as she did the space of two and fortie years) to labour in the vine of holy Religion cultiuating the Palme tree by austere pennances, fastings, disciplines and mortifications before she could gather and tast the sweet fruite of euerlasting happines.

How saint Francis withdrew sainte Clare from the world and made her Religions.

CHAP. XI.

THe Noble Damsell *Clare* the Spouse of *Iesus Christ* wholy distrusting in her owne forces greatly apprehended that her new entreprise would be assaulted and impugned

by

by her friendes and kindred, but calling to
mind that for the atcheiuing of any glorious
enterprise there is no meanes so seeure as to
haue recouse vnto God by holy prayer, he
neuer forsaking those that shroud themselues
vnder the wings of his protection, she began
with intense feruour & the profusion of many
teares to implore the diuine assistāce, knocking
incessantly at the gate of the diuine clemencie
by feruent prayer, she was not frustrated of
her hope. For God who is allwayes pleased
with the prayers of the humble, and doth accomplish the desires of the iust, inclining to
their vowes and supplications destroyed the
force of humaine power: inspiring her the
way and meanes how to effect her holy de-
signes, infusing into her soule an vndanted
courage to incounter the Prince of darcknes;
Wherfore the night following Palme Sunday
the year 1212. the 19. of *March* the 18. year
of her age she began to prepare to accomplish
the command of her spirituall guide and Directour S. *Francis*, and to make a glorious flight
and honorable retyre from the world in mo-
dest company; but it seeming to her impossible
to goe forth at the ordinarie and cheefest
doore of the house, she bethought her selfe
to take the benefit of a back doore which
(though it were dammed and closed vp with
grosse stones and mighty blockes) she with an
admirable courage and force rather of a strong
man then a tender young damsell, her selfe

O   broke

Iudith.
9.

*Chron.p
1.l.8.c.
4.
Wadd.
ad ann.
1212.
§. 21.*

broke open; this then leauing her Fathers
house, her Citie, kindred and Friendes; she departed so priuatly that none had inkling, or
knowlelge therof, and with extraordinary
speed she arriued at S. *Marie of Portiuncula*
which is a quarter of a mile distant from *Assisium*; where the Seraphicall Father S. *Francis*,
with his Religious expected her: they receiued
her with burning wax tapers singing the
himne *Veni creator Spiritus*. This holy Virgin who sought her Spouse and Redeemer
Christ Iesu with Lampe not extinct & empty,
but filled with diuine loue: and incontinently
in the selfe same houre and place, hauing left
and abandoned the impurities ot *Babylon*; gaue
the world the ticket of defiance before the
Altar of the soueraigne queene of Angells,
where the glorious Father S. *Francis*, cut of her
hayre, & then cloathed her with a poore. Habit of the Order: renouncing the Iewels, and
gorgeous attire wherwith she was adorned to
be giuen to the poore to set forth here the de
uotion of her minde, and the abondance of in-
internall graces which she receiued in this ve-
stition, and the vnspeakable ioy of her heart: is
a thing altogether impossible: truly it had not
bene conuenient that this new Order of Florishing virginity should other wise begin, the
in the Angelicall Pal'ace of that great Lady
and immaculate queene who alone was found
worthy to be the mother of God without any
detriment to her virginall purity: wherfore it

was

was most requisite, that in Church dedicated
to her honour (as this of *Hortulana* was,) should
first spring the florishing vine of noble virgins:
in this same place had the noble chiualry of
the poore of *Iesus Christ* the Freer Minors their
beginning vnder the valorous Captaine S.
Francis, to the end it might euidently appeare
that the mother of God in this her habitation
ingendred and produced the one and the other
Religion, choosing S. *Francis* and his B. daugh
ter S. *Clare* for to renew and establish vpon the
earth the spirit of our Lord and contempt of
the world: making the one a Father of most
honorable and illustrious children, and the
other a mother of many virginall daughters,
poore of temporall goods but enriched with
spirituall gifts, and heauenly treasures: this
beautifull and chast damsell hauing receiued
the ensignes of holy penance , was conducted
by the Seraphicall Father to the monasterie
of *Saint Paul* which was of Religious woemē
attired in black, to remaine there till allmighty
God had prouided another Monasterie: now
you may behold this new Spouse of *Christ Iesus*
to enter a fierce and hard combat.

W*add.*
ad annū
1212.
§.21.

*How the kindred of sainte Clare la-
boured to withdraw her from
the monasterie.*

CHAP. XII.

THE Bleare eyed blind world not able to
support so great a light, and the Diuell
fearing that the example of this virtuous
Damsell would worke him some great ouer-
throw resolued to wage warre against her, by
her neerest kindred who most commonly are
the domesticall enemies of Religious persons;
euery one thought it strange that a Damsell of
a noble familie, beautifull, rich, & in the prime
of her yeares, should abandon all pleasures,
pomps, riches, and honours; for to embrace
and vndertake a grosse patched habit vile and
contemptible; and most rigid and austere pennance; they deemed it would be to them a
great affront if their kinswoman *Clare* liued
in this poore estate; which in the sight of the
blind world seemed miserable; wherfore coming to the monasterie of the Religious woemen of S. *Paul* they vsed all the endeauors,
which enraged folly suggested vnto them, to
supplant her holy resolution; first profering
all sort of obsequious seruice, and amiable
friendship and courtesie, next shewing great

Chro. p. 1
l. 8. c. 5.
Luc.
Wadd.
ad ann.
1211. §
22.

rigour

rigour, and vttering menacing threates, and
lastly they attempted by force and violence to
haue carryed her away, being not able to pre-
uaile and surmount her by persuasions, and
trying their strength against the meeke Lambe
of *Christ Iesus*, they sought to intrap & deceiue
the innocent Doue by their malice & wicked
counsell: making her a thousand deceitfull
promises to force her to yeeld and retire from
so abiect and contemptible a life, protesting it
was a thing vnworthy her noble birth, & that
such an absurditie had neuer bene seene in
their Citie: but she with an inuincible courage sayd vnto them: *deare friends and kinsmen,
when God doth speake, the world must be silent and
giue place: and when God doth call, wee must fly to
obey, though to the hazard and perill of a thousand
liues: Christ Iesus hath called me to his seruice, I will
obey him and will take him for the Spouse of my
soule: and neuer will I settle my loue or affection on
any but him:* and to oppose and withstand their
violence, she tooke such fast hold of the Altar
that she drew of the Altar cloathes and vnco-
uering her head she shewed how her haire
was cut of and sayd. *That she could not be separated from the seruice of her Redeemer for whose loue
she had forsaken the world, and them also, and the
more they did vex and tormēt her the more would
her heart be inflamed in the loue of her God who
would minister new forces vnto her to resist and
ouercome.* Thus for many dayes together she
was assaulted with iniuries and reproches, and

S. Clares answer to her kindred.

In the Bull. of her Cannoni-zation

O 3   sustain ed

many great contradictions and oppositions in the way of perfection, and notwithstanding that her friendes were obstinate and perseuerant in diuerting her from her pious resolution, neuertheles her zeale and feruor did not relent nor her courage faint, but on the contrary the contumelies and threats did augment her confidence in God and awake the generosity of her minde, so that in fine they were compelled to desist and retire with shame and confusion, in this sort did our Lord manifest his might and power giuing strength to the weake and feeble to surmount the strong and mighty of this world: some few dayes after she was conducted by our holy Father *Saint Francis* in company of two of his disciples Brother *Phillip* the long and Brother *Bernard Quintauall*, to the monasterie o' the Religious woemen of *Saint angell* of *Panso* of the Order of S. *Benedict* neare to *Assisium*.

Luc. Wadd. ad annū. 1212.9. 23.

How

*How the B. Virvin Agnes was conuerted
by the prayer of her Sister Sainte Clare
and of the persecution she indured
by her kindred.*

CHAP, XIII.

*Chron.p.
1.l.8 s.
6. Luc.
Wad. ad
annum,
1212.
§.28.*

S Ainte *Clare* had a Sister younger then her
selfe, who both in regard of bloud and purity was really her Sister. And she exceedingly desiring the conuersion of her Sister
neuer failed in her feruent deuotions which
she offred to Allmighty God, beseeching him
most feruently that as she and her *Sister Agnes*
had liued together in the world in great loue
& vnion of mindes that he would now cause
betweene them a more perfect coniunction of
wils and profession in his holy seruice, most
instantly beseeching him to make it appeare to
her Sister what a notorious deluder the world
is, and how full of discontentment; and that he
would change her resolution of carnall marryage: and cause her to embrace the vnion of
diuine loue and to take for her spouse the king
of glory. Our gratious Lord made no delay to
fauour this his poore suppliant and deuout
seruant, in this her first petition: sixteen dayes
after the conuersion of S. *Clare* her Sister A-
gnes inspired of God with a strong and resolu-

O 4   te courage

te courage gaue a flip & farwell to the world,
and came to her Sister to whom difcouering
the fecrets of her heart she told her, she was
refolued to ferue God in her company: the
which she vnderftanding moft cordially imbraced her and full of ioy and exultation she
fayd vnto her, *my moft deare Sifter I giue infinite
thankes to our Lord* Iefus Chrift *that it hath plea-
ied him to heare me, and deliuer me from the affliction I endured for your fake, for I feared that you
would haue forfaken the Paradife of virginity, and
haue enthralled your felfe to the flauerie of marryage
preferring a man before God, and earth before heauen;* This noble conuerfion of *Agnes* was fe-
conded by as many contradictions of her kindred as that of S. *Clare*: for the diuell by a cruell
Alarum and fierce affault went about to di-
fturbe and threaten the totall fubuerfion of
the quiet repofe and heauenly confolation of
thefe two virgins, for their kindred hauing
vnderftood that *Agnes* had ioyned her felfe to
her Sifter *Clare* twelue men of their ne ereft
bloud affembled together to affault and wage
warre againft the two Spoufes of *Iefus Chrift*: and
tranfported with extreame rage and furie, dif-
fembling neuertheles at the firft ariuall their
lewd intention : she wing them a fauorable
countenance : then addreffing themfelues to
the virgin *Agnes* difpairing of all hope to withdraw S. *Clare* from her holy purpofe, they
demaüded of her wherfore she was retired to
that place, and willed her to delibe rate and

resolue

refolue to returne with them, to her Father
houfe wherto she anfwered that she was refolued (the grace of God affifting her, to remaine with her, Sifter: which anfwere one o
them difdaining, full of paffion and transported
with choler, tooke her by the haire, and gaue
her many blowes with his feete and fifts: then
vfed all his ftrength to pull her out of the
place which at the length by the help of others
he performed: For taking her in their armes,
they forcibly trayled her out. But this tender
damfell feeing her felfe violently wrefted by
thofe inraged Lyons out of the armes of her
God, began to cry to her Sifter: *help me Sifter
and permit me not to be feparated from our Lord*
Iefus Chrift *and your louing company.* Her carnall friendes trayled along the valley this holy
virgin againft her will, and in defpight of her
moft couragious refiftance pulling of her
haire, and renting her clothes. In the meane
while *Saint Clare* vnable to help her Sifter by
other meanes had recourfe to prayer with a-
bondance of teares, befeeching God to giue a
couragious confidence vnto her Sifter that
his diuine fauour defending his faithfull feruant, humaine forces might be ouercome, and
our Lord hear her: For no fooner had she ended her prayer, but the body of the virgin *Agnes*
became fo weyghty, that her aduerfaries were
conftrained to leaue her on the ground, and
albeit fo many men and their feruants put all
their forces to lift her vp yet could they neuer

doe it, but called labourers and workemen of
the vineyards that wrought thereabouts to
assist them, yet their great number no more
auailed then the lesse: finally all their forces
failing, they acknowledged the euident miracle, though in derision saying it is no meruaile though she be so waignty, hauing layne
eating of lead all night, wher vpon Seignour
Monaldo her vncle in extreame choler, lifted vp
his Arme to strike her, but presently he was
surprised with an extreame paine therin,
which did not only torment him for the present but continued a long time after; S. *Clare*
after her prayer ariuing, besought her kindred
to forbeare in vaine to contend with God, and
to leaue to her the care of her Sister who lay
as halfe dead. They perceiuing their labour lost
to hinder their pious resolution, being exceedingly wearyed, left the two Sisters together:
they being departed *Agnes* arose from the
ground very ioyfull and comforted in our
Lord, for whose loue she had fought and ouercome (in this first conflict) the world, and the
Diuell, and her Sister asking her how she felt
her selfe, the innocent lambe answered her;
that notwithstanding that they buffeted and
beat me with their fistes, spurning me with
their feet and pulling me by the haire, trayling
me through stony wayes, by the diuine help
and the merit of your prayers I became insen-
sible to all the euills which I suffered: the
world is not worthy nor capable to conceiue

the

the ioy and comfort which thefe heauenly
foules experienced after thefe trialls and per-
fecutions, and the breuity of the hiftorie hath
buried in the tombe of filence the fweet and
heauenly difcourfes which paffed betweene
thefe two Sifters who now enioyed but one
heart in two bodies: they contemned and
laughed at the folly and madnes of worldlings
and at the weakenes and impotency of men,
that were not able to ftirre or mooue one yong
damfell only: this did a frefh enkindle in their
breafts a moft intenfe feruour, to facrifice and
dedicate themfelues to the feruice of God, and
to caft afide all feare and apprehenfion of dif-
ficulties whatfoeuer, fith the diuine maiefty
did fo euidently affift them rendring them inuincible: this heauenly fauour did make ferene
and calme the ftorme and tempeft which was
raifed in the heart: of the chaft Turtle *Agnes*.

How S. Francis *gaue the habit to* B. *Agnes, and of the dignitie of the Monafterie of Saint Damian.*

CHAP. XIV.

S *Aint Francis* inflamed with the loue of
Soules, hauing heard the noble conftancie
and generous refolution of B. *Agnes*, and

the reproches and torments which she had
constantly endured of her kindred: moued
with a zeale of her soules saluation, inflamed
with perfect Charity, and illuminated by God,
hastened to the monasterie of S. *Angell of Panso*
where she was in the company of her Sister
S. *Clare* he layd open vnto her the deceipts
and inconstancie of the world; the impurity of
carnall pleasures, and the malice and treacherie
of the Diuell, exhorting her to forsake riches
for voluntary pouerty, to macerate her body
by austere mortification of the flesh, brideling
the disordinate appetites therof by fasting and
disciplines: renouncing her owne will by an
intire abnegation of her selfe: whilst this
fortunate Damsell was attentiue to these
wholesome instructions, the holy ghost
wrought so powerfully in her soule by his forcible inspirations that she was constrained to
yeeld her selfe captiue to allmighty God, submitting her selfe to his directions, feeling
in her Soule the inflamed dartes of diuine
loue, loging after nothing but heauenly things.
Wherefore the Seraphicall Father, to satisfy
her desire, cut of her haire, and cloathed her
with the habit of the Order like her Sister:
leauing her her owne name of *Agnes*, in memorie of the innocent lambe *Christ Iesus*, who
offring himselfe in sacrifice to his Father, Redeemed the world with the price of his pretious bloud. And truly *Agnes* lead a life wholy
conformable to her mysterious name. For she

*Chr p.1.
l.8 c.6.
Luc.
Wad.
ad annu
1112.§.
24*

was

was meeke as a Lambe, and a true Doue without gall, her innocent life was more Angelicall
then humaine, she was white and resplendant
by her virginall purity, fruitfull in virtue, ad
orned with all perfection: patient in pennance
and sicknes: obedient to her guide and directour S. *Francis*, sacrificing her selfe to her
Redeemer as a Paschall Lambe on the tree
of the Crosse in labours and austerities of holy
Religion and strict Euangelicall pouerty,
from the age of 14. yeares til she was deliuered
and set free from the Captiuity and bondes of
her bodie. But by reason that S. *Clare* and B.
Agnes her Sister could not find their hearts
content, nor enioy with perfect repose the
sweet embracements of their heauenly Spouse
according to the feruour of their mindes, a-
mongst the Religious woemen of *S. Beneaicts*
Order, they were conducted by their directour
S. *Francis* to the Church of *S. Damian* ioyning
to the City of *Assisium*: Fastning in that place
the anchor of their generous resolution. S.
Damian is a Church which S. *Francis* laboured
much to repaire in the beginning of his conuersion, and where he offered his money to
the Chapline for to repaire it. In this same place
praying with great effusion of teares he merited to heare the voice of the Crucifix, which
three times reiterated vnto him: *Goe Francis*
and repaire my house, which, *as thou seest,*
c *ready to fall*; this is the place wherin S. *Clare*
mprisoned and shut vp her selfe from the

Petrus
Rodulph
fol. 136.

Luc.
Wadd.
ad annū
1212. §.
25.

P 3   tem

tempestuous turmoiles of this world, building
her nest like a siluerd doue in the clifts of this
Church, renewing the Colledge of sacred
Virgins: giuing a beginning to the Order of
poore Ladyes: and being entred into the way
of pennance she bruised the hard turfes of her
members with the coulter of the Crosse:
sowing the seed of all sanctity, becomming a
perfect mirrour and bright glasse to direct
those in deuotion that were to follow
her through this sacred desart and sweet so-
litude.

How Sainte Clare *by her example and renowne hath drawne many daughters after her,*

CHAP. XV.

THE fame and renowne of S. *Clare* running more swift then any Post, was presently diuulged : so that many damsells
in imitation of her, drew neare vnto *Iesu Christ*
sacrificing vnto him the inestimable pearle of
ther virginity: marryed woemen indeuored to

liue more chaſt and virtuoſly, gentle woeme n and Ladies contemning their faire houſes and ſumptuous tables ſhut vp them ſelues in mo naſteries, eſteeming it a great glorie to liue in ſtrict pennance for the loue of Ieſus Chriſt. This Saint was alſo a ſpurre vnto men, to excite in them a violent feruour, and principally youth that beganne to take courage in the conte mpt of the world, and by example of the frailer ſex to fight againſt the temptations and deceiptfull pleaſures of the fleſh; many marryed perſons with mutuall conſent obliged them ſelues to continency, the men entring into monaſteries of men, and woemen into monaſteries of Re-ligious women, the mother induced the daughter to ſerue Ieſus Chriſt, the daughter the mother, one Siſter another: and briefly each one by a holy enuy deſired to ſerue. God, and to participate of the Angelicall life which was demonſtrated vnto them by this holy damſell: in ſuch ſort this little plant of S. *Francis*, as a fruitfull tree ſprouting forth into ſundry bowes and branches, hath ingendred a copious linage & ſo great a familie that they couer the whole earth.

For the conſolation of thoſe who are de-uoted to S. *Clare* we will ſet forth to their view ſundry Religious woemen, famous for ſanctity who floriſhed in S. *Clares* time. We will giue the preheminence and firſt place to B. S. *Agnes* who merited the ſpirituall fauour to be her eldeſt daughter and her true Siſter

both

Chron-
p. 1. l. 8.
c. 6.
Luc.
wad. ad
annum.
1153 §.
23. 24.

both by bloud, vertue, and Religion: from the time she entred in to the monasterie of *S. Damian* to the day of her death she wore a rough Cilice, subduing her flesh by the asperity ther of, her ordinarie repast was most commonly bread and water, she was of a disposition very pittifull to all, for her vertue she was a paragon and paterne of all perfection: she hath founded seuerall monasteries in the strict obseruance of the Rule: and in fine hath bin famous for miracles before and after her death B. *Beatrix* Sister to *S Clare* hauing forsaken the riches of this world at the age of 18. yeares followed to Religion her Mother *Hortulana* and her two Sisters *Clare* and *Agnes* entring in to the monasterie of S. *Damian* wherin she liued Religiously in fasting, watching, and praying, finishing her life with renowne of great Sanctity.

Chron.
p.2.l.1.
c.33.
Luc.
wad.ad
annum.
1253.§.
15.

B. Sister *Pacifica* neare kinswoman to *S. Clare* who in the world had accompanyed B. *Hortulana* in her deuotion of visiting the holy Land, she was compleat in all virtue, merit and perfection, she was sent by *S. Clare* neare to the valley of *Spoletum* to a place called the *valley of glory* there to erect a monastery according to the intention of *S. Francis* in Regular obseruance, she was highly fauored by God. For being wholy destitute of water where she built her house, she fell to prayer with her Religious, there appeared within the precincts of the conuent a faire great Hinde which open-

Chron. as
a boue
Luc.
wad. ad
annum.
1213.§.
64.

ing

ing the ground with the hoof of his foot, frō whēce inståtly sprung vp a chriſtalin foūtaine, which continueth to this day; many oppreſſed with ſundry maladies are cured by the drin king of this water.

B. Siſter *Ayme* couſſin of S. *Clare* by whoſe prayers ſhe forſooke the vanities of the world ſeruing God in her company in the monaſte- rie of S. *Damian* imitating her rare vertues. Her purity, and innocencie of life, was ſo ad mirable that ſhe merited to ſee *Ieſus Chriſt* at the death of S. *Clare*, when ſhe ſayd vnto her, my deare daughter *Ayme* doe you not ſee the King of glory whō I behold? and immediatly the eyes of Siſter *Ayme* were opened and ſhe beheld her heauenly ſpouſe, by whoſe ſights ſhe became more feruent in his holy ſeruice, per- ſeuering in the exerciſe of vertue, ſhe in fine repoſed in our Lord.

Chron. as aboue Luc. Wadd. ad annum. 1213. §. 65.

B. Siſter Balbina couſſine to S. *Clare* and Si- ſter to the aforeſayd Siſter *Ayme* in imitation of the Sainte forſaking all vaine and deceipt- full delight of this world entring in to the ſame monaſterie where ſhe arriued to ſo high perfection, that by many miracles her worth and merit was made manifeſt. This ſer- uant of God was ſent by S. *Francis* to found ſundry monaſteries.

Chron. as aboue Luc. Wadd. ad annū. 1215. §. 36.

B. Siſter *Chriſtina* liued in the houſe of S. *Clare* being her intimate friend and priuie to all her actions when ſhe viſited the ſeraphicall Father S. *Francis* hearing and receiuing from

Chron as aboue Luc. W ad. ad annum. 1213. §. 66.

Q him

him the sacred instructions of her conuersion; and in imitation of her, she went to S. *Francis* at our Ladyes of Angels where she receiued the Habit and in it the space of 44. yeares she followed the steps of the glorious Saint in the perfect obseruance of her holy Rule. B. Sister *Agnes* of *Aßißium* endewed with the simplicity of the Doue she merited to see *Christ Iesus* in the forme of a little child, cherishing and dandling S. *Clare* and as she doubted of the verity of the vision she heard a voyce directed to her saying: *In medio eorum sum*: I am in the midst of them, an other time she receiued this admirable fauour to behold the holy Ghost descending vpon the Saint in forme of a fierie beame:

B. Sister *Francis* was of a most perfect life, she saw our Redeemer in the forme of a beautifull yong child sit in the lapp of S. *Clare* vpon S. *Phillipp* and *Iacobs* day,

B Sister *Benauenta* liued most Religiously with S. *Clare* the space of 26. yeares: she saw the sacred virgin mother of God comming to the bed of S. *Clare* the day of her death: louingly embracing her, as wee shall recite heerafter.

B. Sister *Benedict* was a Religious of so great prudence, Sanctity, and perfection, that after that S. *Clare* was receiued in to the heauenly glory by her Spouse: she was elected Abbesse of S. *Damian*: and gouerned that monastery in the obseruance of Pouerty, and being come

Luc. Wad. ad annum. 1213. §. 67.

Luc. Wad. ad annum. 1213. §. 68.

Luc. Wad. ad annum. 213. §. 18.

Luc. Wad. ad annum. 1214. §. 74.

to

to the ēd of her dayes, she passed happily to her Greatour being adorned with many miracles. She is buried in the quire of the Church of S. Clare in Aßisium, and she is held in great veneration.

The B. Sister *Balbina*, *Clare* and *Agnes* cossins of S. *Clare*, cōming miraculously to *Barcelone*, with Sister *Anastasia*, Sister *Philipp* of *Aßisium*, Sister *Cecilie* of *Spoletum*, and Sister *Lucie* of *Rome*; all true disciples of the diuine *Clare*, as true followers of the vertues and perfections of their holy mother, haue bene adorned with great Sanctity, exemplar life, and many miracles.

B. Sister *Clare* of the noble familie of V-*baldinie* in the life of S. *Clare* gouerned the monasterie of mont-*Celse* in *Florence*, after that S. *Agnes* was returned to S. *Damian*, for the greater consolation of her Sister; this Lady, before she was entred into Religion was marryed to Signour *Galet* one of the most illustrious gentlemen of all *Florence* she hauing considered the sanctity of life of the aforesayd Religious, their manner of life so pleased her as she forsooke the world, and her two children, and shutt vp her selfe in that monasterie, there to serue her heauenly spouse *Christ Iesus*: two of her neeces called *Iane* and *Lucie* Sisters to O-*ctauian Vbaldinie* Cardinall in her company, enrolled themselues amōgst this new florishing company; the Cardinall her nephew through the great loue he bare to his Aunt and his two

Luc.
Wad. ad
annum.
1214. §.
34.
annum.
1233.
§. 35.
annum.
1253. §.
9. annū.
1315.

Chron.
p. 2 l. 1.
c. 54.
Luc.
Wad. ad
annum.
1261.
§. 7. 8.
9. Pe-
tr. Ro
dulp. fol.
137.

Sisters,

Sisters, considering the dangers and perils
wherevnto this monasterie was exposed, by
reason of the continuall wars , he caused a
Conuent to be builded within the Citty of
Florence neare to the Roman gate called *Saint
Peter Gatoline*, wherfore the yeare 1261. the
Cardinall hauing ordained a solemne procession , he introduced the forsayd Religious to
the number of fifty; bringing with them the
bones of the Religious men and women who
had bene interred in the forsayd monasterie, a
Cloke of S. *Francis*, and the Stole wherwith he
sung the Ghospell celebrating the Natiuity of
our Redeemer, neer to the Cittie of *Crecio*: and
a sacred veile which S. *Clare* gaue vnto them
at her death: our souueraigne Redeemer by a
notable miracle, made manifest how pleasing
this procession was vnto him; for all the bells
of the Cittie of Florence, did ring of themselues, without any humaine helpe, continu-
ing this melodie, votill such time as the sacred
Reliques were with reuerēce reposed in their
due place: this B. Sister *Clare* reposed happily
in our Lord leauing behind her a most sweet
Oiour of vertues, she is buried in a Sepulcher of marble, twelue yeares after her Sepulcher being opened to burie her neece, therin
her bodye was found as entire, faire and sweet
as if she had bene but newly dead, and as they
lifted her vp in her tombe, she lifted vp her
right hand giuing therwith her benediction,
to a great number of people there present: two

                                                hundred

hundred yeares after, she was againe found entire, her flesh being as found and sweet as if she had bene but newly departed without the least corruption of her garments.

B. S. *Agnes* daughter of *Orets* King of *Bohemia* inspired of God tooke the Habit, and made her profession of the austere Rule of *S. Clare*, this Princesse sent a messenger expressely from the Citie of *Prague* to *Assisium*, to render Obedience to *S. Clare*, as to her true mother and Superiour, the B. Sainte returned back vnto her most gratious letters sending vnto her for a token a cord, a veyle and a cup of wood with a dish, wherin she was accustomed to eat and many such small things, which the Princesse accepted with singular deuotion, our Lord wrought many miracles by the sayd things, which haue euer bene conserued in the sayd monasterie with great reuerence: this noble Princesse being adorned with many vertues and miracles, hauing assembled many Religious women into diuers monasteries, in fine she left this transitorie life, to goe to enioy the eternall in company of her glorious spouse, she dyed in the Citie of *Prague* the yeare *1285.* the Emperour *Charles* the fourth was twise deliuered from death by the intercession of this noble Princesse, wherfore at his death he commanded his Sonne and successour, in the empire Wenceslaus to prosecute her Canonization: but he being hindered by continuall hard and difficile warres, could

Chron.
p. 1. l. 8.
c. 40.
Luc.
Wad. ad
annum.
1354.
§. 4.

not execute the pious desire of his father: wherfore she was frustrated of this honour as well as many others, who haue not receiued this from men in the militant Church being most glorious in the triumphant, for a great volume would not be sufficient to set forth the liues of the Religious women of the Order of S. *Clare* renowned for sanctity and miracles.

Chron.
p.x.l.8.
c.4t.
Luc.
Wad.ad
anpum.
1241.§
4.5.6.
Petrus
Rodulp.
fol. 136.

B. Sister *Helena* of *Padua* florished in great sanctity & perfection in the monastery, which was erected by S. *Francis*, in the Citie of *Padua* where S. *Anthonie* rendred vp his Soule to God: but in as much as the hearts, of the seruants of God, are as Anuils which are alwayes hammered on and liue by the blowes of afflictiós, she was proued by Ie*sus* Chri*st* & refined like gold, in the furnace of aduersitie, for she lay in her bed depriued of her corporal health, her sight, and her speech, the space of fifteene yeares, manifesting by exteriour signes, an admirable ioy and alacrity of heart; our Lord reuealed many secrets to this Sainte, which she manifested to the Religious women: who caused them to be carefully written, to record them to posterity: for by signes she could very well expresse to the Religious, what she desired: her body till this present remaineth entire her face and contenance is deuout, young, and beautifull: her teeth fresh and white as is if she were but new dead, when there is any Calamity likely to befall the Citie the body of this

virgin

virgin doth ſtirre and moue in her tombe, with a mighty ſound and noiſe: which is the cauſe that the inhabitants of *Padua*, doe immediatly apply themſelues to pious workes, to prayer, faſting, Almesdeedes, & Pennance to appeaſe the wrath of God, and to diuert from their Citie, the warres, Peſt and famine, with other diſaſters; which hang ouer their heades: if you deſire to know, yet more of theſe true diſciples and imitatours of S. *Clare*, who are without number, euen in S. *Clares* life-time; you may pleaſe to looke wher theſe marginall annotations doe direct you.

Luc. wad. to 1. and 2. Petrus Rodulp. fol. 137. 138. 139. 140. 141.

Monaſteries which were built in S. Clares time.

CHAP. XVI.

SAinte *Clare* the little plant of S. *Francis* did alſo ſee the banner of her Order, to floriſh and fructify, extending and ſpreading her branches ouer all Chriſtendome. Italie the earthly Paradiſe of the Church, doth glorie to haue brought forth ſo many goodly ſtockes or Families.

That of *Saint Damian* of *Aſsiſium* is the Lady, queene, and Empreſſe of the whole Order.

Perugia is one of the moſt ancient, it was builded by *Agoline* Cardinall Protector of the

Perugia Luc. wad. ad annum. 1218, § 13.

Order,

Order, who was afterwards Pope, by the name of *Gregorie* the IX.

The Citie of *Aretie* caused to be built a goodly monasterie which was gouerned by B. *Balbina* (daughter to Seignour *Martin* of *Carano* cosin to *Sainte Clare*) according to the perfection of the Ghospell and intention of *Saint Francis*.

Padua hath had the honour to see *Saint Francis* lay the first stone of the monasterie of the poore *Clares: Florence* built the monasterie of *mont Celie* at the very same time

The Holy Citie *Rome* hath presented vnto her, the goodly monasterie of *Cosme, and Damian.*

Venice hath bin adorned with a faire monasterie of poore Clares, enioying *S. Agnes* the Sister of *S. Clare* for her foundresse,

Mantua doth glorie that it enioyed a Conuent in *S. Clares* time, and had *S. Agnes*, her Sister for the first Abbesse therof.

Bologna, solicited by *Arnould* Protectour of the Order, who was after Pope *Alexander* the fourth: consecrated a goodly monasterie vnto her.

Spoletum hath done the like, and *Milan, Siena, Cremone, Pise, Bergame, Alexandrie, Ascolie*, and many other Citities.

The Roman Empire hath with great admiration beheld her Eagle, to hatch and produce Eagles, which haue afterwardes nursed and brought vp the most rich and illustrious Prin-

ceſſes

Aretie.
1215.
§.36.
Padua.
1220. §
5. 1231.
§.32.
Florence
1221.
§.20.

Venice.
1234. §.
6.

Mantue
1238.
parag.
26.

Bologna
1152.
parag 29

cesses of its Empire, & worthy to haue match-
ed with the highest soueraignty in the world,
S. *Agnes* of *Bohemia* before mentioned the
yeare 1237. which was more thē fifteene yeares
before the death of S. *Clare,* sent vnto her an
honorable Embassage, beseeching her most
humbly to send vnto her some Religious
women, of the monasterie of S. *Damian,* to
gouerne and direct many damsells who with
languishing desires aspired after that heauenly
manner of life: she in the meane time causing
to be erected a Conuent in Prague the Capi-
tall Citie of the Kingdome of *Bohemia* ; the
fame and renowne of this Princesse being diuulged ouer all *Germanie* many monasteries of
poor Clares, were presently founded both at
Trent, Wormes, Sefflingen, Colen, Nurenberg,
Fullingen, and in many other places; S. *Clare* to
comply to the request of this noble Princesse
Agnes sent vnto her certaine Religious women
of most holy and exemplar life, to found and
gouerne the sayd house in the strict obseruance of the Rule and Pouerty both in *Bohemia*
and *Germanie.*

Twenty yeares before the happy death of S.
Clare, the Catholick Kingdome with great ioy
receiued her Religious, who arriued there by
the guide of the Almighty: for the yeare 1233.
the Saint cōmanded two of her kinswomē to
wit Sister *Agnes* and Sister *Clare* her cosins, to
take shipping for *Spaine,* there to found and
erect monasteries; they came vnto *Barcelone* in

Luc.
Wad. ad
annum
1212.
parag.
14.
1150.
paragr.
12.

Luc.
Wad. ad
annum.
1233.
parag.

R   a little

a little Barque without failes, Oares or sterne paffing the dangers and perils of the mediterranean fea, hauing God only their mariner and guide, the inhabitants of the Citie amazed at the nouelty and admirable accident, and confidering the integritie and holy fimplicity of thefe modeft and young Religious Women, and beholding their poor and contemptibl attire, they receiued them into *Barcelone*, as Angells fent from heauen, giuing vnto them the Church of S. *Anthonie* for their dwelling: in imitation of them, great number of Damfells cōfecrated the ineftimable pearle of their virginity, to the heauenly fpoufe; profeffing the fame Rule, erecting many monafteries principally in the famous Citie of *Salamanca*, *Valodelia Bourges* and *Zamora*; and other places.

Salmāca Luc. Wad. ad parag 19 Valode. lid. 1251 paragr. 65. Bourge. annum. 1118. parag. 13 idē 1254 parag. 7. Zamore 1229. pirag. 32 Wad. ad an. 1254 parag. 33 Ierom. Plat. l. 2 c. 27.

The noble flowerdeluce did not only receaue this happy light, but placed it neare vnto her Royall Citie, contributing thervnto of her owne ftemme, the more to innoble and augmēt the lufter therof: for the Lady Ifabella Sifter to S. *Lewys* King of France; & the Lady *Iane* daughter to the King of *Nauarre*, contemned the world and dedicated vnto God the deare pledge of their virginity in the Conuent, near *Paris* called long *Champa* a yeare after the glorious deceafe of the Sainte: wherby wee may gather that the fayd Conuent was built before her death, the like honour hath bene afforded to the monafteries of *Rhemes*, *Bordeaux*. *Mont-Pelliere*, and many other places.

Of

*Of diuers great Princesses who be-
came Religious woemen of the
Order of* sainte Clare.

CHAP. XVII.

NOT without great reason may wee sing
with the kingly Prophet; warbling this
melodious note, A*dducentur regis virgi-
nes post eam*: wee know very well that according to the letter this is spoken of the sacred
mother of God, who by pronomination or ex-
cellencie hath acquired this Epithet of honour and sublime prerogatiue to be the virgin
of virgins: for that she was the first who made that noble Vow giuing therby a rare exam
ple, to all vertuous damsells, to present to the
heauenly King their virginall purity, a Iewell
of inestimable worth (till then vnknowne in
in the world) by that generosity to purchase
the noble crowne of Virginity. I doubt not
but the same may be diuulged to the prayse of
the refulgēt Sunne of virgins in her time B. S.
Clare, sith so many millions of deuout Soules
with great ioy and alacrity of spirit, haue dedicated themselues to God: and admiring the
resplendent Rayes of her supereminent graces,
haue contēned the pleasures of this world, to
imitate the perfections of this noble Lady: vn-

*Psalm.
44.*

der whose instructions they voluntarily enrolled themselues: taking her for their watch-Tower, and bright torch, which should lighten and direct them: whilst they flote on the surging waues of this dangerous and vnconstant Sea, yea many Princesses haue refused the most honorable and aduantagious allyances in the world, for to bind themselues, according to the example of her pouertie, to an austere life, humility and other mortifications.

I will not be from our purpose to produce some of the greatest Ladies of the world, who haue made themselues more famous and illustrious by embraceing this poore reclused life, then by their noble extraction.

Chron. p.
1. l. 8. c.
40. Luc
Wad. ad
annum.
1234.
parag. 4

     B. *Agnes* aboue mentioned daughter to the King of *Bohemia* was promised in marriage, to the Emperour *Fredericke* the second. but she refused to consent, dedicating her virginity vnto God in a monasterie at Prague of the Order of S. *Clare* which she had erected, the Emperour vnderstanding that his Espouse, had forsaken the world: at the first incounter, he was much disquyeted, but after reflecting that she had not forsaken him to ioyne her selfe to any other Prince, but for *Iesus Christ*, before whom all the Kings of the earth are as wormes poore, naked, and miserable, he rested satisfyed, and well edifyed. Her Father intending to assigne a good pension, and rent to the monasterie of his daughter to prouide for the

temporall

temporall neceffities therof, she refifted thervnto, very conftantly: defiring to liue and
dye poore, and to be mantained of Almes ,con-
formable to the Rule: obferuing very exactly
the intention of the Seraphicall Father S.
Francis concerning the vow of Pouerty: the
daughters of many Kings, Princes, Dukes, Ear-
les and other great Lords in *Germanie*, haue
forfaken the world, and the vanities therof
following the footfteps of *S. Clare* and this
noble Princeffe *Agnes.*

 Iane daughter to the king of *Nauarre* more
efteeming the Kingdome of heauen then of
the earth, confecrated her felfe to God, in the
monafterie of *Long champ* to the admiration
of many. *Iffabella* Sifter to *S. Lewys* King of
France fought and required in Marriage of
Prince *Conrard* fonne to the Emperour *Fredericke*, chófe rather to facrifice the puritie of her
Royall Lilly, and the vermillion Rofe of her
virginity to her heauenly fpoufe, then to ble-
mish her Chriftaline purity: wherfore the
yeare 1154. renoúcing the vaine pomps of the
world, defpifing all earthly Diademes, she re-
clufed her felfe in the monafterie of *Long-chãp*:
with fuch feruour of fpirit and fanctity of life,
in regular obferuance: that God hath fealed
her holines with a number of miracles:

 Blanche her neece daughter to *Philipp* King
of France, did in like fort dedicate her virginity vnto God, in the fame monafterie the
yeare 1316.

Luc.
wad. ad
annum
1254
paragr.
42.

annum.
parag.
33 *idem*
1260
parag.
60.

Chron.
p. 2. l. 7.
c. 32.

Chron.
p.2.l.8.
c.49.
Ierom.
Plat.l.
2.c.27.

The Lady *Sancie* queene of *Sicilie* and *Hie-tusalem* a few monthes after the death of *Ro-bert* her Husband cōtemning all worldly great-nes, and Courtly honour, renouncing all, she shrouded her selfe in a monasterie of poore Clares in the Cittie of *Naples*; where this Prin-cesse was so great a louer of humility, as she besought the most B. Father Generall of the Order, that he would please strictly to prohi-bit all her Sisters in Religion, that none of them might call her queene or Lady *Sancie* but simply Sister, the name common amongst all Religious.

Wad. ad
annum.
1219.
parag 6.

Kunegunde daughter to Andrew King of *Hungarie*, and Sister to S. *Elizabeth* the widdow; hauing liued in matrimonie the space of forty yeares with *Boleslaus* the chast King of Po-land, both of them keeping their virginall pu-rity vnspotted; after the death of her Husband she became Religious of the Order of S. *Clare*; she dyed the yeare 1292. and was famous for many miracles.

Luc.
wad. as
aboue.

Her Sister *Ioleine* after the death of her Husband *Boleslaus* the pious Duke of *Cracouie* and Prince of *Poland* vndertooke the same course of life.

Luc.
wad. ad
annum.
t25 4.
parag 37
1268.p.
4.5.6.

Salome daughter to the Duke of *Cracouie* and Sister to *Boleslaus* the chast, hauing liued many yeares with her Husband *Coloman* King of *Galatie*, preseruing the integrity of her virgi-nity, in the state of matrimonie, after the death of her Husband, she receiued the sacred veile,

from

from the Bishopp of *Cracouie* and became a
poor Clare: her fanctity was made manifeſt by
many miracles which God wrought after her
death.

Helena daughter to *Alphonſus* the third
King of *Portugall* became Religious of the Order of S. *Clare*: she was indowed with rare
humility and ſingular charity towards the ſick.
One day a ſickly Siſter deſiring ſome cherries,
she went and gathered ſome greene from the
tree (it being too timely to haue ripe ones) and
preſented them in an inſtant wholy ripe to her
ſick Siſter who eating of them recouered her
perfeſt health; she ended her life adorned
with rare perfeſtion and was illuſtrious for
miracles.

Conſtancia wife to *Peter* King of *Arragon*
and neece to the Emperor *Fredericke* the ſecõd,
after the death of the King her Huſband; she
embraced with great feruour the life of a
Poore Clare.

The ſame courſe haue imbraced *Euphemia*
daughter vnto *Rodulphus* the Emperour: *Agnes*
daughter vnto *Lewys* the Emperour *Blanch*
daughter to the King of *Nauarre*: *Magdalene* Siſter to *Francis* the moſt mighty Duke of *Brit-
taine*: *Iane* and *Marguerite* daughters to *Godfrey*
the moſt illuſtrious duke of *Brabant*; *Marguerite*
and *Agnes* daughters to *Frederick* Duke of *Lorraine*: *Paula* the wife of *Iohn Francis* of *Gonzago*
Firſt Marquis of *Mantua*.

Philip of *Gueldres* of the noble and Royall

*Petr. Ro
dul. fol.*
141.142

*Luc.
wad. ad
annum.*
1259. p.
18.

*Luc.
wad. ad
annum,*
1290.
*parag.*21

houſe of *Bourbon* Ducheſſe of *Lorraine* and *Bar.*
&c. after the deceaſe of *René* King of *Sicile* her
huſband ſhe applyed her ſelfe to the workes of
piety and deuotion, and in fine wholy forſooke
the world, the more freely to ſerue her Creator, entring in to the Conuent of the Poore
Clares of *Ponte a Mouſſon*, obſeruing exactly
the Rule, the ſpace of 27. yeares, in great feruor of ſpirit and ſanctity of life, neuer admit-
ting of the leaſt diſpenſation, ſhe rendred her
happy ſoule into the handes of her Creator
the yeare 1547. and of her age 85. leauing
behinde her a fragrant Odour of her ſweet
virtues, and the reputation of a great Sainte.

The Ladye *Marguerite* of *Auſtrie* daughter to
Maximillian the II. Emperour and to *Marie* Siſter to *Phillip* the II. King of Spaine; Siſter to
Rodulphus, and *Mathias* Emperours, and to *Al-
bertus* the Arch-Duke of Auſtrie, and Duke of
Brabāt, &c. Being ſought in marriage of ſūdry
great Princes, notwithſtanding ſhe contemning all worldly greatnes and terrene pomp,
choſe rather to be an abiect in the houſe of
God conſecrating her ſelfe to his diuine ſeruice in a monaſterie of S. *Clare* where the rigour
of the Rule is moſt exactly obſerued. Truly this
is a rare & notable example, to behold ſo great
a Lady and Princeſſe, to humble and debaſe
her ſelfe, to ſo poore and abiect a habit, contenting her ſelfe with a Cell of 7. foote long,
and 5. broad, tying her ſelfe to continuall faſting, and to many ſtrict obediences and hard

mortifi-

mortifications: neuertheles this noble Lady of **Austria** doth esteeme her selfe more honored by this vocation, which by the inspiration of God she hath vndertakē, &boūd her selfe vnto wher in she laboureth to become more illustrious by the greatnes of her eminent vertues, most curiously elaborated and perfectly ingrauen in her soule, then by the splendour of her noble ancestours.

Of the humilitie of sainte Clare.

CHAP, XVIII.

PRofound humility was the first assured stone, and foundation layd by this prudent virgin, in her beginning in Religion, after she had begunne to labour in the way of God: being not ignorant how this virtue in perfection, is the Regent and gouuernesse of good workes, the treasurer of merits, the foundation of all virtue: she was not puffed vp with the smoke of vaine glory, (a poison most easily swallowed, and fed by good workes themselues) for being Foundresse of so many monasteries, and mother of an innumerable number of Daughters: for she gouerned by holy Obedience, trembling vnder the burthen of vaine worldly dignities: truly it is a great

Vaine-Glory a pleasant and dangerous poison.

S   folly)

folly to glory in honour, and Superiority, for which wee shall one day pay a deare price, sith that *of him that hath receiued much, much shall be required*: and as all proceedes from God so should all be referred to him: and he doth not deserue to receiue any new benefit, who maleuoloufly doth attribute to him selfe, what totally apertaineth vnto God, all proceeding from the inexhaustible foūtaine of his immenfe liberality: She was very dexterous & difcreet, in concealing the heauēly fauours, and that in fo fweet, and innocent a maner, as it was moft remarkable: making not the leaft fhew of what had happened. If Obedience or charity did vrge her to folace the afflicted, after she had prayed to our Lord with great feruor imploring his affiftance, she fent them to her mother Sifter *Hortulana* or to fome other Religious womē confpicuous for Sainctity, that to them might be attributed the cure and whē any one would referre the honour to her, she vterly denyed it, vfing this ordinarie fleight: faying, if I could cure the ficke, I would folace my felfe, for I ly languifhing fo many yeares but cannot dye, would I (thinke you?) be fo inconfiderate as to cure others, and permit my felfe to remaine and perifh in my miferie? after this fort *humble Clare* the more she was adorned with Celeftiall gifts, graces, and miracles, the more she ftill depreffed and humbled her felfe; to the defcent of her owne nothing, keeping all thefe heauenly fauours

locked

locked vnder the key of humble modestie,
within the sacred Closet of her heart, neuer
desiring of other Herauld to publish her per
fections, then a most profound silence, stifling
vaine glory which doth ly hid in the very
center of the soule, and often doth lurcke
vnder the most refined spirituallity, if infati-
gable diligence be not vsed to expulse it. Her
greatest ambition was to be seruant of ser
uants, at the feete of all, and the lowest of all;
and for no honour which was euer done vnto
her did she euer digresse from this humility
wherin her heart was settled : her attire was
poore, and humble, her exercises were abiect
lowly and contemptible, and finally her speech
was deuoid of all selfe conceipt reputeing her
selfe as a worme of the earth. She disdained
not to execute the office of a seruant washing
of the feete of her Religious and seruing them
at the table, when as she commanded any thing
it was with great repugnance, desiring rather
to obay then to command, she exhibited to the
sicke all kind of seruice how vile or abiect
soeuer cleansing the loathsomest and fowlest
immundicities, she often washed the Feete of
the lay Sisters when they returned home from
begging and wipeing them she kissed them
with great deuotion: one time it chanced that
washing one of their Feet which she embraced
but the Sister refusing that act of humility
withdrew her Feet, but she did it so rudely
that she gaue she Sainte therwith a great dash

Chr.p.1.
l.8.c.7.
Luc.
Wadd.
ad annū
1215.§.
38.

on the face, yet so farre was the virgin from being offended therwith that on the contrary she mildly tooke the Foot of the Sister againe and kissed the sole therof: thus did this true Espouse of *Christ Iesus* accomplish the doctrine of her Maister and the example which he left when he washed the Feete of his Apostles. An act of great note which happened in her presence doth shew the great reckoning she made of humilitie; An English Freer Minor, and Doctour in diuinity preaching at the Monasterie of *S. Damian* in the presence of *S. Clare*, and of B. Brother Giles the third disciple of *S. Francis*, a Lay brother by profession, and indewed with an admirable simplicitie and sanctity of life, he desired (as a zealous fried of humility) to make tryall of the sayd virtue in this Preacher, therfore in the middest of his Sermon he willed him to be silent for that he himselfe intended to Preach: immediatly the diuine gaue ouer and Brother Giles with great feruour propounded most high and sublime matters to the great astonishment of his audience, then turning him selfe to the diuine he willed him to prosecute his discourse, wherevnto he obayed: which *S. Clare* beholding exclaimed with ioye and exultation: this day is fulfilled one of the cheefe desires of our Seraphicall Father *S. Francis* who often reiterated saying: I desire my Religious should be so humble that a Doctour in Diuinity intending to preach should giue ouer at the word of a

simple

I oan. I 5

Chron. p 1. l. 10. c. 12.

simple lay Brother and giue him the place:
I assure you my deer Sisters this preacher
hath more edifyed me then if he had raysed
the dead.

Of the perfect obedience of S. Clare.

CHAP. XIX.

THe glorious Virgine S. *Clare* had in sin
gular recommendation the virtue of holy Obedience produceing the example
of the sonne of God of whō the Doctour of
the Gentiles sayth, *Iesus Christ* hath annihilated
himselfe taking the forme of a Seruant: becōming obedient vnto death, yea the death of the
crosse submitting himselfe to so hard an obedience as to vndergoe the most scandalous ignominious and painfullest death in the world:
the little and humble seruant of God *Clare* hauing vowed obedience to S. *Francis* did allways
perseuerantly bow vnder the yoake of his cōmandement in most plyable and obedient manner, respecting the person of God in him and
esteeming him as the interpretour of the di
uine will: she vnfolded to him the motions
of her heart with an Angelical purity listening
attentiuely to his instructions and exactly ful
filling his commandes as if they had bene di-

Chron.
p.1.l.8.
c.7.
Luc.
Wad.ad
annum.
1215.§.
28.

uine Oracles: three yeares after her conuersion
through great humility she desired to obay ra
ther then command, to be a subiect rather then
Superiour, to serue amongst the handmaides of
Iesus Christ rather then to be serued: she most
humbly besought the Seraphicall Father to re
lease and free her from the chardge and title of
Abbesse, and to make her the lowest in the
house wherunto he would in no sort consent:
but commanded her for obedience and charity
to continue the same : she knowing very well
that to obay is requisit to haue feete to runne
wings to fly and handes to execute whatsoeuer
the Superiour doth ordaine bowed her shoul
ders to the burthen and accepted the chardge
denying her owne will: which ingendred in
her soule more feare then presumption wherby
she became rather subiect then free. S. *Francis*
sayd one day vnto her: my daughter prepare
your selfe to goe whither soeuer I wil send
you, she made answere with great humility &
submission as a true child of obedience, Father
dispose of me as you please I am yours I
haue consecrated my will vnto God, it is no
more my owne, I am ready to goe whither
soeuer you thinke conuenient: a noble sentence
worthy of S. *Clare*, and to be well imprinted
in the heart of euery Religious persō, reducing
to their minde how on the day of their Profes
sion by the vowe of obedience they haue so
dispoiled themselues of their owne will that
they haue no more right thervnto: and if they

Luc.
Wadd.
ad annū
1212.§.
32.

call

cal it backe vseing it at their owne liberty the^y are proprietaries before God vsurping by aⁿ_o irregular act what they had consecrated t^o God by their Profession.

Of the pouerty of Sainte Clare, *and her great zeale to this virtue.*

CHAP, XX.

OVR Redeemer *Chriſt Ieſus* intending to lay the foundation of the new Hieruſalem deſcending from heauen: in his admirable ſermon on the mountaine began by the recommendation of Pouerty, B. are the Poore of ſpirit: giueing her the firſt place, as to her that beggetteth all other virtues, for truely Monaſticall Pouerty doth quite banniſh and take away all cares and incombrances which doe depreſſe a man: it is the direct way to heauen, the expulſer of ſadnes, nurſe of peace: and the beeſome which doth cleanſe the ſoule from all tranſitorie cares: finally it is the ſollid foundation of all Euangelicall perfectiō taught and practiſed by our Redeemer: in whoſe handes are all the boundes of the earth, and yet he had not one foote of ground where to retire him ſelfe: vpon this perfection hath the Catholick Church beene grounded by the A-

poftles profeffed enemies to riches, fo as the
firft and principall of them all making open &
publicke profeffion of this Pouerty fayd, gold
and filuer I haue not. Perfection wheron our
Seraphicall Father hath fecurely piled his Order, cherrishing her as a moft noble Orient
pearle: ftileing her his Mother, Miftreffe, Ladye, and Queene: vpon this perfection his holy
difciple and eldeft daughter *S. Clare* would
plant and eftablish her Religion: for in the beginning of her conuerfiō she caufed her whole
inheritance and patrimonie to be fold refer-
uing nothing to her felfe: difpoiling her felfe of
all tranfitorie riches to facrifife them at the
foote of the Crucifix, hauing in this fort exteriourly abandoned the world, and interiourly
inriched her foule she ranne after her beloued
far more lightly being freed from the burthen
of terrene things: she contracted fo ftrict an
amitie with holy pouerty and became fo ena-
moured therof, as she would enioye nothing
but naked *Iefus*, neither would she permitt.
her daughters to poffeffe any other riches, and
with this Euangelicall trafficke she purchafed
the ineftimable treafure of Celeftrall Beatitude
in lieu of all other things which she had fold,
acknowledging that the fame could in no fort
be enioyed together with the diftraction and
occupation of temporall things: inftructing her
Religious she would often fay vnto them that
their company would be then gratefull vnto
God when they were moft rich in Pouerty,

and

and would be conferued most firme and stable
if it were allwayes fortifyed and inuironed
with the rampiers and strong bulwarkes of
pouerty: she allso admonished her beloued
daughters in *Chriſt Ieſus* to conforme themſelues to him lying poore in the bed of pouerty,
and being but newly borne was by the moſt
ſacred virgin his Mother layed in the manger:
and in his life poſſeſſed nothing liuing of continuall allmes, and dyed wholy naked on the
Croſſe. His deuout ſoule receaued with great
ioye and comfort the peeces and morcells of
bread which the Religious men brought from
the doores: hauing demaunded it for the loue
of God, shewing no ſuch content at the ſight of
whole loaues. She would neuer heare of rētes,
reuenewes, penſions, or any ſtable poſſeſſions.
Pope Gregorie the ninth louing this Eſpouſe
of *Ieſus-Chriſt*, with a fatherly affection, arri-
uing at *Aſſiſium* the yeare 1228. for the Canonization of the Seraphicall Father *S. Francis* be
fore he made his entrie into the Citty he went
to viſitt his deer daughter *Clare*, and amongſt
other diſcourſes he laboured to perſwade her
to admitt of rents, alleadging the great viciſſi-
tude and alterations of times, warres, incur
ſion of Enemies, and pilladge of Countries, the
coldnes of Peoples deuotion towards the
poore of *Ieſus Chriſt*, the pouerty and miſerie
of the world; wherfore he iudged it conuenient she should be eſtabliſhed in ſome ſecuri-
ty by rents and poſſeſſions, he proferring him

T   ſelfe)

felfe to beſtow them vpon her ; but all theſe
waighty reaſons and faire offers ioynéd with
the ſoueraigne authority of ſo great a Prelate
were not of force to make her conſent or cháge
her vndaunted reſolution , wherfore the Pope
ſayd vnto her my daughter if you feare to
breake or infringe your vowe I will abſolue
you from that obligation ; but the couragious
virgin anſwered him preſently with great pro
foũd humility moſt holy Father I ſhall be euer
glad to receaue from your holineſ the abſolu-
tion of all my ſinnes ; but I neuer deſire to be
abſolued from following the pathes and ſteps
of my Redeemer *Chriſt Ieſus*: many Prelats and
great perſons came to viſitt her who counſeiled
her to mitigate her Rule in the point of pouerty and auſterity; but after ſhe had well way-
ghed the affaire and recommended the ſequell
to God ſhe fully reſolued to obſerue the firſt
Rule which had bene giuen her by the Seraphi-
cali Father S, *Francis* conſidering that our Lord
would giue ſufficient ſtrength and forces to
thoſe whom he ſhould call to this B. ſtate and
happy condition to vndergoe it : to conclude:
all her care and cheefe ſtudie was in all the degrees of perfect pouerty to conforme her ſelfe
to naked *Chriſt* crucifyed , ſo that no terrene
thing ſhould be able to ſeparate the poore virgin from her beloued nor impeach her from
running after the ſweete Odour of his per-
fumes.

How

How Sainɕe Clare demaunded of Pope Innocent the forth the priuiledge of pouerty.

CHAP. XXI.

Chron. p. 1. l. 8, c. 8. Luc. Wad. ad annum. 1251. §. 7.

MAny priuiledges are dayly fought for and demaunded of the foueraigne Bifhopp, but neuer hath the like to this bene heard of which the prudent virgin and humble fuppliant *Clare* did feeke for: for defiring to intitle her Religion with the title of pouerty, she demaunded of Pope Innocent the fourth the priuiledge of pouerty: to haue pouerty for her patrimony pouerty for her confolation, pouerty for the folace of all her diftreffes and pouerty for the fundamentall ftone of her Order: his holines who had neuer heard fuch a demaund or bene prefented with the like fupplication amazed at her generous refolution and admirable couftancy auoutched publickly before the Cardinalls, and the whole Court: that the like priuiledge had neuer bene demaunded of the Sea Apoftolick: neuertheles he highly extolled her magnanimous requeft: and fince she defired with her daughters to lead an Apoftolicall life he graunted her fuit and to the end a new & vnacuftomed fauour might comply with a new requeft the Pope with great content writt with his owne hand

T 2　　　　the

the firft letter of priuiledges, watering it with teares of deuotion.

The Bull of Pope Innocent the fourth how the Religious of Sainte Clare may not be conftrained to receaue rents or poffeffions.

I Nnocent Bishop feruant of the feruants of God to his deerly beloued daughters in *Iefus Chrift:* Clare Abbeffe and the other Sifters of the monaftery of *S. Damian* at *Affifium,* as well prefent as to come health and Apoftolicall benediction; feing that it is manifeft that you haue fold all your goods to beftow them on the poore the better to renounce the thoughts and defires of temporall things defiring to be wholy dedicated vnto God, and that you haue a firme refolutió not to hold in what fort foeuer any poffeffions or immoueable goods following in all things the footfteps of him who for vs was made poore the way the truth, and the life; neither is the neceffity and want of temporall things able to terrifie you from this firme purpofe for fo much as the left hand of your heauenly fpoufe is vnder your head to fuftaine the great feeblenes of your bodye the which you haue fubiected vnto the law of the fpiritt with great feruour of charity

that

that Lord who feedeth the birds of the air and
cloatheth the hearbs of the feilds will reward
you with himselfe in eternity : when his right
hand shall embrace you gloriously in his perfect vision. Mooued heerwith as allso for that
you demaund of vs with great humility that
wee would confirme vnto you with our Apostolicall graunt: the sayd resolution which you
haue taken to follow the most high pouerty
wee yeeld vnto you by the tenour of these present letters, that you may not be constrained
by any whosoeuer he be, to haue, take, or re-
taine any temporall possessions: and if any mayd
would not or could not keepe this Rule let
her not remaine with you but be straight way
sent vnto some other place : also wee ordaine
and forbid that no person of what quallity or
condition soeuer he may be, be so bold as to
trouble your monasterie : and if any person Ec-
clesiasticall or secular knowing this our consti-
tution and confirmation, attempt in what sort
soeuer to doe contrary to the same, and after
hauing bene three diuers times reprehended
and aduertised, doth not amend and make due
satisfaction for his fault, he shall be depriued
of his office, dignity, and honour : and that
one may knowe such a person allready to be
condemned for his wickednes by the iust iudgment of God, he shall be cut of from the holy
communion of all faithfull Christians and
shall be guilty of the diuine vengeance at the
last iudgment: but those who loue you all in

Chrift

Chrift Ieſus, and your Order, ſpecially the monaſtery of *Saint Damian*; the peace of God be
with them, to the end they may receaue the
fruit of their good Workes and may find the
recompence of eternall beatitude at the day of
the rigorous and laſt iudgment.

Of the great prouidence of God towards S.
Clare.

CHAP. XXII.

IT is a notable draught and ſigne of the ſingular prouidēce of God that ſo many poore
Religious not reſeruing any temporall
goods nor ſo much as the freedome or power
to wish or deſire againe thoſe goodes which
they haue renounced and abandoned by an ex-
preſſe and voluntary vowe: wholy relying on
the ſuccour of the diuine prouidence, doe yet
neuer want nouriſhment or neceſſarie main-
tenance for this life: It is a couenant and com-
promiſſe of mutuall obligation, (according to
the ſaying of S. *Francis*,) made betweene God
and the Religious: to wit that the Religious
for their part ſhould forſake and abandone all:
and our Lord for his part ſhould maintaine
and nouriſh them, and that not in the nature
that a Maſter doth his ſeruants: but as a Father doth his Children: it appertaines to the

soue-

foueraigne prouidence of God, to prouide the
of all things necessarie: which his pietie per-
formeth with such assiduous care, as if he tooke
a singular delight therein. On this diuine
prouidence the prudent virgin *Clare* hath founded her Order, Religion, and Familie. It shall
not be from our purpose, to record two miracles, which did spring from the merits of this
zealous louer of pouerty. One day, it chanced,
that there was not in all the Monasterie one
loafe of Bread, and the houre of dinner being
come, the Sainte called the *Dispenser* which
was Sister *Cecilie* of *Spoletum*, and appointed
her to diuide the loafe in two, and to send halfe,
to the Religious Brothers, who serued with
out, and reserue the other halfe for themselues:
whereof she should make fifty portions, because there were so many Religious: and that
she should lay them on the table of pouerty:
wherevnto the *Dispenser* answered: that the
miracles of *Iesus Christ* were needfull to make
so many portions forth of so small a quantity
of bread, but S. *Clare* replyed, my daughter doe
what I bid you. The Religious woman went
presently to effect the commaund of her Abbesse: who went to prayer with all her Religious, presenting their vowes and teares to
their heauenly Spouse, and immediately, by
the diuine goodnes, the small peeces of bread
did so augment in the handes of the *Dispenser*
that cutt them, that they suffised for the refection of the Community. This was a stroake

of

of the paternall prouidence of God, who
was in this fort delighted to confolate
thofe who ferued him , with fo free a hart. It
happened an other time that the feruants of
Iefus Chrift wanted oyle , fo that they had not
fufficient to dreffe meate for the ficke : *S. Clare*
being aduertifed of this neceffity , tooke a pott
which (as Miftreffe of humility) fhe wafhed
with her owne handes : then fent it to the
Turne-wheele : to the end a brother might
goe begg fome for the loue of God : the B.
Damfell recommending this want to the
prouidence of God : the Religious brother
being called found the fayd pott miraculoufly
full of excellent oyle : wherfore thinking that
the Sifters had called him without neceffity,
murmuring to himfelfe, he fayd , thefe Sifters
knowe not what they would haue , their
pott being full of pure oyle. God did in this
fort often prouide by extraordinary meanes
for the neceffities of his poore hand maydes
by the interceffion of their prudent Mother.

Of the auſtere mortification faſtes and abſtinence of S. Clare.

CHAP. XXIII.

Lthough the Bodye hath beene giuen
vnto the ſoule for a deer and inſeparable
companion to be her ſubiect and without reſiſtance in all things to obay her will;
notwithſtanding after the ſinne of our firſt Father, ſhe is become rebellious, and violating
the bandes of amity is turned into a fierce and
cruell enemy, refuſing to be ſubiect to any but
her diſordered appetites, ſeeking eaſe and delight in ſenſuall pleaſures, flying mortification
abſtinence and pennance and all acts of virtue
this tirant doth euer wage warre againſt reaſon
precipitating her in to many vnworthy acts;
wherfore it is requiſite to chaſtiſe the rebellious fleſh, humbling and ſubduing her by auſterity, pennance, mortification and ſtripes,
vſing her in Nature of a ſlaue teaching her to
obay the commaundements. Of reaſon, in this
ſort did S. *Clare* triumph, for ſhe was ſo ſeuere
and in ſome ſort cruell to her owne bodye: as
to her deadly enemie, her life was no life but
a life of continuall faſting, neuer deſiſting for
her infirmity or any other occaſion how vr-
gent ſoeuer. She cloathed her innocent body

V with

with one single habitt all patched and a cloake
of grosse cloath rather to couer her body
then to defend it from the importunities of the
seasons, neuer wearing stockings nor shoos to
defend her selfe from the cold; this Espouse of
Iesus Christ inuented new wayes to cloath her
selfe with the liueries of her spouse for she
caused to be made a tunick of hoggs haire
which she wore next her skinne, this was
not sufficient to asswage the heate of her loue
nor satiat the desire she had of doing pennance
for she wore besides a Cilice made of horse
haire interlaced with hard knotts, which once
Sister *Agnes* of *Assisum* borrowed of her with
great importunity but hauing experienced the
sharpnes therof she restored it to S. *Clare* more
readily then she had ioyfully borrowed it, admiring how so tender a body could support it;
her ordinary bed was the bare ground vsing
some times to lye vpon the cuttings of vignes
and a block of wood for her bolster or pillow;
she rent her body with cruell and hard discipli-
plines; by these feruorous austerities subduing
the flesh and preseruing the lustre of her virginall purity: but in regard that the rigorous life
wherwith she afflicted her body brought her
to sicknes, the holy Father S. *Fran* is commaunded her to lye vpon chaffe: the rigour of
her abstinence in her sastes was such that she
could not maintaine her body in life so little did
she eat, wherefore it was apparent that she
was sustained by diuine virtue: when she had

                                              her

her health she fasted from all Saints to Christ-
mas and the whole Lent with bread and water
except the Sundayes: and which is more admirable three dayes in the weeke to wit,
Munday Wednesday and Fryday in the
Lent she eat nothing at all, and the better to
dispose her selfe for the fastes commaunded by
the Church on the Eues of the sayd fastes she
eat nothing but bread and water; wherfore
wee need not wonder if such a rigour so long
continued bred many infirmities in this holy
virgin extenuating her forces, and ouerthrow-
ing the naturall vigour and health of her body,
the deuout Religious daughters of this holy
mother had exceeding compassion of her bit-
terly lamenting the vntimely death which she
voluntarily procured her selfe , for remedy
wherof S. *Francis* and the Bishop of *Assisium*
forbad her those three dayes of fast which euery weeke she inflicted on her selfe , and commaunded her not to passe one day without taking at the least anouce and a halfe of bread to
conserue life ; and allbeit such greeuous afflictions of the body doe accustome to breed
allso some affliction to the heart, yet in her it
produced a contrary effect, for her coūtenance
was euer mild and ioyfull in all her austerities,
so as she seemed to haue no feeling of them or
to feare no inconuenience by them, setting light
by all corporall afflictions which sufficiently
demonstrated that the spirituall ioye wherwith
she was interiourly nourished appeared exte-

riour y in her holy face ; becaufe the true loue
of the heart maketh pennance fweet and
eafy.

How Saint Francis *and* Sainte Clare *made their refection together and of an admirable rapt.*

CHAP. XXIV.

THE chaft and vnfpotted Turtle *Clare*
was fingularly deuoted and affected to
the Church of Portiuncula it being the
place where she had giuen the tickett of de-
fyance to the world before the Alltar of the
fouueraine Queene of heauen and earth con-
fecrating her felfe to *Iefus Chrift* her immortall
Spoufe ; therfore she feruently defired to vifit
once more this facred chappell wherunto *faint
Francis* condefcended not without the diuine
infpiration who intended to worke great matters by this holy conference. This holy virgin
accompanyed with fome of her Religious Sifters entred into this holy temple, wher a long
time she prefented her prayer vnto God, yeelding him thankes for the fauours which she
had receaued in that place, she faluted her Ad-
uocatreffe the glorious Queene of Angells;
and vifited all the Alltars S. *Francis* going forth
of the place, ordained a napkinne to be fpread

on the ground with a slender portion according to his pouerty: for the first messe he began so highly to discourse of diuine mysteries
that both himselfe S. *Clare* and all the Religious
men and woemen there present were rapt in
extasie, their eyes eleuated on high and their
soules in a manner transported to heauen: at
the same instat the Cittizens of *Assisium* beheld
the house of our Lady of Angells to burne and
all the bordering place and mountaine adiacent
but aboue all the fire ouer the monasterie seemed most raging and vehement wherfore they
hastened from all sides to quench it, but comming to the place they found neither fyre nor
flame but only of the holy ghost whom they
considered and acknowledged in the counte-
nances and aspects of those whom they found
yet sitting absorbed in God with S. *Clare*, and
her companions, from whence awaking and
perceauing the heauenly grace they tasted little
els, being allready saciated and full of this spirituall food: thus euery one retired yeelding
thankes to God, who doth present and afford
himselfe to those who doe vnite themselues to
him by Charity S. *Clare* returned to her Monastery of S. *Damian* wher her Religious receaued her with singular consolation beeause they
feared S. *Francis* would haue sent her to found
a Monasterie in some other place as he had
done to her Sister *Agnes* to whom he gaue the
gouuernement of the Monastery neer *Florence*
and this they apprehended the more for that he

had warned her to be ready to goe whither
soeuer he should thinke fitting.

*The coppie of a letter which S. Agnes
writt from Florence to her Sister
Sainte Clare , and to all
the Religious of S.
Damian.*

CHAP. XXV.

TO the venerable and beloued Lady and
Mother in our Lord *Iesus Christ Clare* &
to all her Conuent humble Sister *Agnes*
the least of the disciples of *Iesus Christ* and of
yours, commendeth her selfe vnto you all and
prostrate at your feet doth yeeld you all submission and deuotion, wishing vnto you what
is most pretious from the most high king of
kings , to the end that all nature that hath bene
created of God doe acknowledge it selfe to be
such as it cannot persist of it selfe in its owne
essence the diuine prouidence most prudently
permitteth that when any one esteemeth him
selfe to be in prosperity then is he drowned &
plunged in aduersity: this I tell you my most
deer mother that you may knowe what affliction and extreame heauines possesseth my spirit being so tormented that hardly can I speake

and

and this becaufe I am corporally feparated frõ
you and my holy Sifters with whom I hoped
to haue happily liued and dyed in this world fo
far is this my greefe from flacking that it continually increafeth which as it had a beginning
fo doe I beleeue it will find no end in this
world; for it is continuall and familliar vnto
me that I greatly feare it will neuer forfake
me I was perfwaded this life and death should
be a like without power of any feparation vpõ
earth amongft them who haue one fame con-
uerfation and life in heauen and muft haue one
fame fepulture, them I fay whom one fame e-
quall and naturall profeffion and one fame loue
hath made Sifters, but fo farre as I can fee
being abandoned and afflicted on each fide, I
am much miftakē O my holy Sifters, I befeech
you to be reciprocally greeued with me and
lett vs weep together being affured that you
shall neuer experience any dolour like vnto
that which I now feele in being feparated frõ
them with whom *Iefus Chrift* had conioyned
me, this greef tormenteth me inceffantly
this fier burneth my heart continually fo that
being on each fide afflicted I know not what
to thinke neither doth any hope remaine but to
be affifted by your prayers that allmighty God
eafing this afflition may make it tollerable
vnto me: O my moft gratious Mother what
shall I doe, and what shall I fay, fith I know
not that euer I shall fee you more or likewife
any Sifters that it were lawfull for me to vtter

vnto you the conceipts of my soule as I would
desire, or that I could open my heart vnto you
vpon this paper then should you see the liuely
and continuall dolours that torment me , my
soule burneth interiourly being afflicted with
an incessant fyer of loue, and my hart groaneth
sigheth and lamenteth with desire of your presence, myne eyes can not haue their fill of weeping and albeit I seeke for some consolation
against this bitternes yet can I find none but e-
uery thing turneth in to greefe , and much
more when I consider the meanes to see you
I am intirly steeped in these anguishes, hauing
none that can comfort me in this life , but that
I receaue a little consolation from the liberall
hand of our *Sauiour Iesus Christ* which causeth
me to beseech you all to giue thankes vnto his
diuine Maiesty, for this fauour and mercy extended towards me : and for that through his
grace , I find such concord , peace, and charity,
in this conuent as by words can not be expressed, these Sisters hauing receaued me with exceeding loue and deuotion, yeelding me Obedience with extraordinary promptitude and
reuerence , they all with one accord recommend themselues to our Lord *Iesus Christ* , and
to you my Sister , and to all the Sisters of the
monasterie, and I recommend my selfe and
them to your holy prayers, beseeching you as a
mother to be mindfull of them and of me as of
your daughters, and know you that they and I
will all the dayes of our life obserue and keepe

your

your holy preeepts and aduertiſemēts , beſides
I deſire you ſhould know that the Pope hath
accorded to whatſoeuer I demaunded of him
conformably to your intention and mine particularly in the matter you know; to wit that
wee may not poſſeſſe any thing proper , I be-
ſeech you my moſt dear mother to procure the
Reuerend Father Generall that he often viſit
vs, to comfort vs in God, whoſe grace be with
your ſpirit. Amen.

Of the great deſire Sainte Clare *had to
ſuffer martirdome for the
loue of her Creatour.*

CHAP. XXVI.

THe Angelicall Doctour *S. Thomas* who
is held to be one of the greateſt and pro-
foundeſt deuines that hath appeared in
this world and a bright ſhining ſtarre in the
Church of God is of opinion that there is not
in our Chriſtian Religion any act more great
more noble excellent and meritorious then the
excellency of martirdome , in ſuch ſort as he
exalteth the triumph of martyrs aboue the dignity of confeſſours and virgins , or aboue any
other degree of merit ; and truly not without
iuſt ground, ſith *Ieſus Chriſt* hath firſt giuen his
ſentence in fauour therof: ſaying ther is no   *Ioan.*15

X   greater/

greater testimonie of true affection and loue to
a friend, than to expose his owne life to▪ him
this is performed by the glorious martirs giuing proofe of their great zeale to God to the
losse of their liues: which they expose like generous champions for the loue of their Creatour. S. *Clare* vnderstanding that fiue Religious
men of the Order S. *Francis* the yeare 1219 had
receiued the palme of martirdome by Marmolin King of Marocho a great persecutour of
Christians and that the Seraphicall Father had
blessed the monastery of Alenquer (from whence
they were departed to goe vnto martirdome)
with his benediction, be thou blessed the habitation of the most high which hast begot &
brought forth to the king of heauen fiue beautifull flowers of the colour of the Rose and
bloud, and of a sweet and most odoriferous
sent; that is fiue true Freer Minors the first
fruits of this Order; that for euer the Religiõus
who dwell in thee obserue most exactly our
Rule, she therfore being animated like a noble
Elephant by the beholding of bloud shed for
the loue of God, her heart was so feruently inflamed and set on fire, that she breathed nothing but martirdome and the effusion of her virginall bloud, desiring to become wholy like
vnto her Spouse who was white by innocency
and Ruddie and purple in his bloud; all her
prayers and communions tended towards the
obtaining of this feruerous desire of her soule,
wherfore in imitation of the Religious before

men

Luc.
Wadd.
ad annũ.
1215.§.
36.

mentioned defiring to shew vnto erring and
ignorant foules the true way of faluation, not
regarding her owne weaknes nor the frailty of
her fex she refolued to paffe the feas and to
feeke out the king Marmolin, and for the exe-
cution of this her generous defigne she prefented fupplication vpon fupplication to the
holy Father *S. Francis* befeeching him to giue
her licence and permiffion : but the prudent and
pitifull Father commaunded her to furceafe
and to fuppreffe the feruour of her interiour
motions, perfeuering in her conuent, declaring
vnto her that her long life and prefence was
alltogether needfull, fith she was ordained in
the Pallace of the great king for guide and miftreffe of his deare Efpoufes : & that in her monafterie she was to vndergoe, a long, teadious,
and painfull martirdome : as fince hath bene
truly verified : fith for the fpace of two and
fortie yeares with a Magnanimous and inuincible courage, she vnderwent pouerty, renun-
ciation of her owne will, continuall fafting,
difcipline, and a life moft auftere, with continuall ficknes and corporall infirmity wherwith
she macerated her flesh without all mercy or
pity, contemning her aduerfarie and all his
temptations triumphing ouer him : crucifying
the flesh with the concupifcences therof, by
this meanes gaining a glorious victorie of martirdome. The Seraphicall Father *S. Francis* hauing receiued the impreffion of the facred fti-
gmates difclofed that fingular fauour to his

eldest daughter in *Christ Iesus* S. *Clare* shewing
them vnto her and she made him certaine plaisters to mitigate his dolour : some of these
plaisters are yet reserued in the sayd Conuent
of Religious Women in *Assisium* in great ra-
uerence.

How Saint Francis *gaue his benediction* to Sainte Clare *before his death and his body was shewed vnto her after his* decease.

CHAP. XXVII.

THe faithfull seruant of God *saint Francis*
knowing that the time approched wherin he should render vp his soule to his
Creatour: being sick in the City of *Assisium*
he desired to be carryed to our Ladyes of Angells: that he might yeeld vp the spirit of life
where he had receaued that of grace : and hauing obtained licence of the Bishop , and Gouernour of the City he caused him selfe to be
carried being accompanied with great part of
the City : and being come to the hospitall
which is in the midde way betweene the City
& *Portiuncula*, causing himselfe in his bed to be
layd downe on the ground and turning himselfe

to

towards *Aßisium* he befought God for the
People and the Citie, and wept forfeeing the
great euills and warres which were to befall
it and gaue his benediction faying: be thou
O City bleffed by the fouueraine Lord God,
becaufe by thee many foules fhall be faued, &
many great feruants of God of both fexes fhall
dwell in thee, and by meanes of thee many fhall
paffe to the king of glory, after his benediction profecuting his way to our B. Lady of
Angells, *Sainte Clare* his true difciple and deare
daughter in *Iefus Chrift* fearing not to fee him
before his death, fet a Meffenger vnto him how
fhe was in the fame extremity, and that fhe
could not liue long yea perhaps fhe fhould
goe the firft, and that fhe felt inexplicable
griefe to dy without his benediction, and
without the comfort of his prefence, he being
her Maifter and beloued Father, wherfore
with bended knees fhe befought him by the
facred Paffion of our B. Sauiour that he would
not let her thus depart deuoid of comfort, but
graunt her this laft and fingular fauour as to vifit her before he went to our Lady of Angells,
the Seraphicall Father *S. Francis* felt himfelfe
moued with the bowells of fatherly compaf-
fion for that he could not fatisfy her for the
eminent perill wherein he was and for that the
Phifitions knights and gentlemen who did
tend him would not permit him: calling for
penne inck and paper he fent her by a Religious man his benediction and then lifting vp

X 3 his

his eyes to heauen he sayd vnto him goe and
comfort my beloued Sister *Clare* giuing her
these good tidings that she shall see me before her death and it shall be soone, and all her
Sisters likewise to their great consolation. This
prophesie tooke effect : for after his death the
Religious, Clergie, Priests, and multitude of
people carried him with all piety, reuerence
and deuotion to the Religious of *S. Damian* to
the end they might see and behold this holy
body imbellished and adorned with the sacred
woundes of our Redeemer, and that they
might giue him the last imbracement.

It is not to be expressed what content S.
Clare and her Religious Sisters receiued beholding the body of their holy guide and directour : adorned with the fiue diamants and
pretious pearles of his sacred woundes, wherfore S. *Clare* brake forth into these wordes : O
God most admirable in the person of our holy
Father S. *Francis*, sith thou hast honored him
to beare the markes of thy sacred passion, the
badges of thy crosse, the woundes and scarres
wherby thou hast redeemed the world and
gained a most glorious and triumphant victory.
O my daughters how happy are our eyes
which doe merit to behold the sacred stigmats
which God with his owne handes hath impressed in the handes of our beloued Father : O
thrise happy are our lipps wherwith wee are
permitted to kisse the woundes of his handes :
and Feet, and that of his side florishing like a

fresh

fresh vermillion Rose O sacred woundes first indured by the sonne of God for our sinnes. and now renewed in our Seraphicall Father for our sakes S. *Clare* with her Religious hauing honoured and kissed the fiue vermillion Roses of his woundes, watered and bathed his body with their teares: she laboured (but in vaine) to haue taken out one of the Nailes forth of the wound of his hand to haue conserued it for a pretious Relicque wherfore she contented her selfe to dipp a cloth into the woundes of the Father which is to this day kept with great deuotion in the Conuent of S. *Clare* in *Assisium*: she measured the height of his body and caused him to be drawne in liuely colours, which picture she placed in the Oratorie of her Religious the body was restored to the people who were much wearyed with their long stay he was carried to S. *Georges* and buried in a new tombe where he remained foure whole yeares vnder sure custodie vntill a Church was built to his honour, at the despence of Pope *Gregorie* the ninth, he himselfe laying the first stone in the presence of a multitude of people, if you desire now to know the posture of this B. body, it is in a Caue or Chapell vnder the ground, standing vpright on his feet without any stay, his face turned towards the east, his eyes lifted vp to heauen looking very attentiuely as he was accustomed in his life time, his handes ioyned one within the other within the sleeues of his

Luc. Wad. ad annum. 1218. §. 19.

Luc. Wad. ad annum. 1230. §. 4.

hab

habit resting on his breast: in all parts his body is as entire & free from corruptiō as at the first day of his death : nothing being lacking vnto him but speech and motion: his woundes and the bloud of them are exceeding fresh in this posture and manner Pope *Nicolas* the fifth with six other persons did find him the yeare **1449** which was **223** yeares after his death, he yeelded so sweet and fragrant a smell that scarsely could they support it for it was so admirably penetrating that it raysed their spirits into extasie.

Of the spirituall doctrine wherwith Sainte Clare *nourished her daughters.*

CHAP, XXVIII.

THis vigilant Abbesse *Clare* was not ignorant how the care of soules is great perillous, and dangerous , in such sort as the most virtuous and most sufficient finde themselues oppressed therwith often sighing and groaning vnder the burden of their office, as accountable to God for the soules of their subiects, according to that saying of the Apostles : Obey your guides and be you subiect to them for they watch ouer your soules as those that must render an account for you before the

ad Heb. 13.

face

face of our Lord: an Angell guardian hath but
one soule in his custodie, and yet he hath often
enough to doe, but a superiour hath as many
soules as he hath subiects. For which cause this
prudent prelate *Clare* did often seeke to haue
freed her selfe from the chardge, but obedience
and charity forced her to bow vnder the yoake
of superiours she shined in the middest of her
daughters like a most refulgent sunne by the
light of her holy doctrine and the splendour of
her good workes: coupling together doing
and teaching; her toung, and her handes, her
words, and her workes. The daughters did
behold themselues as in a glasse in the life of
their mother labouring to doe as she did, and
in imitation of her they indeuored to aduance
in the loue of their heauenly spouse, darting in
secret toward heauen most sweet and amorous
affections sufficiently declaring that they delighted in nothing but heauenly things after
which they incessantly breathed by the powerfull attraction of their Superiours incitements
he that would haue seene an Abridgment and
model of perfection might haue looked on the
Conuent of S. *Damian,* where the loue of God
and obedience to Superiours did rule, all the
Religious being Angells, and amiddest the hell
of this world was to be found a Celestiall pa-
radice. She taught them to cleer their soules
of all rumors of the world that they might the
more freely attaine to the high secrets of God:
and not to adheare with disordinate affection

Chron.
p.1.l.8.
c.7.
Luc.
Wad. ad
annum.
1215. §.
38.

Y to)

totheir kindred but to forgett the house of their Father to be gratefull in the eyes of *Christ Iesus*; she admonished them to surmount and contemne the necessities of their bodyes, and to gett a habit of repressing the deceipts and appetites of the flesh by the bridle of reason: she allso instructed them that the subtill enemy armed with malice continually addresseth his hidden snares to surprise pure soules, and that he tempteth the pious in an other sort then worldlings; finally she would have the howers of the day well deuided, part to be employed in prayer and the other part in corporal labour being an Enemy to disordered tedious and too long deuotions, as being the feruours of self loue and feigned holines. After the Canonicall howers she ordained that her Sisters should be employed in handy-labours the more to incite them againe to prayer, and by these occupations were inkindled in their breastes fyrie dartes of diuine loue, she had such a winneing and allureing conuersation that she rauished the hearts of her Sisters, none euer heard her speake but it mollifyed their hearts, others dissolued into teares before her like snow by the powerfull beating of the sun beames: neuer was ther seene a stricter silence then there, nor a more Angelicall manner of life there was not in this holy house to be seene one sole act of vanitie neither in word, nor signe; nor any lightnes of Idle discourses, so mortifyed they were. *S. Clare* had not onely a care of the soules

of her daughters but allso of their weake and
tender bodyes prouiding for their necessities
with great zeale and charity, for she went ofte
in the night when it was cold to visit and couuer them when they slept, and if she found any
benummed with cold or otherwise in ill dispo
sition through the strict obseruance of the cōmon rigour she commaunded them to take
some recreation till such time as they had satisfyed their necessity: when this meeke Doue
saw any of her Religious assaulted with tēptatiō
or with melancholie she called her aside and
louingly comforted her : and often times cast
her selfe prostrate at the feet of those that were
afflicted with sadnes or sicknes to mitigate the
force of their greefe by her motherly cheri-
shings : for which they prooued not vngratfull, but surrendered themselues deuoutly into
the handes of their holy mother , they reue-
renced the Office of Prelacie in their Mistresse
and followed the paths of so diligent a guide,
squaring their actions by this Espouse of Iesus
Christ , admiring the excellency of her sanctity
and charitie.

Of the great desire she had to heare the word of God.

CHAP. XXIX.

THis Glorious sainte tooke singular content in hearing the word of God, knowing very well that vnder the rind therof is hid the sweetnes of spiritt, she knew very well that sermons did greatly profit soules denouncing the B. way to eternity to the hearers and as a good appetite and to rellish meate is a signe of good health, and giueth sufficient testimonie of the good disposition of the body: euen so he that delighteth to hear the word of God in sermons or spirituall discourses, hath an assured signe of good disposition and health of soule, the nutriment of the spirit is the word of God : if it be neglected or reiected the soule is not able to liue being depriued of her Food. Wherfore this wise and diligent mother prouided by the meanes of deuout preachers nutriment for the soules of her Religious, she felt an vnspeakable comfort in her heart in hearing the word of God, and alwayes noted and drew out some point from the sermon for her owne aduancement in perfectiõ, reioycing deuoutly in the memorie of her heauenly spouse _Christ Iesus._ Once on a time hearing brother _Philipp_

Chron·p
1.l.8. c.
17
Luc.
Wadd.
ad annū
1251·§.
27.

of

of **Adrian** a famous preacher, there was seene standing before her a beautifull young child who remained with her all the time of the exhortation comforting and cherishing her with great delight Sister **Agnes** of **Assisium** enioying the sight of this vision receaued in it so great sweetnes of spirit that she was not able to expresse it by words, and albeit she had neuer studied yet did she much delight to heare a learned man preach drawing from it the marrow and substance, which she subtilly obtained and tasted with much more gust: she accustomed to say that the sermon of whosoeuer preaching the word of God, was exceeding profitable to soules, considering that it is no lesse prudence to know how some times to gather beautifull and sweet flowers from amongst grosse and sharp thornes, then to eat the wholesome fruit of a good plant. Pope *Gregorie* the ninth prohibited once at the instancie of certaines Prelates that no Religious mā should goe preach at the monasterie of the poore Ladyes without his owne expresse licence, wherat the pitifull mother much lamenting, because that from thēce forward her daughters would seldome be refectionated with spirituall and holy doctrine, wherfore weeping she sayd let them take from vs the Religious men who labour to get vs our temporall maintenāce since they depriue vs of those who giue vs the sustenance of our spirituall life: and indeed she sent to the Prouinciall Minister the Brothers

that

that were deputed to serue and begg for the
Monasterie: refusing to haue Religious to
seeke them bread, since they depriued them
of those that gaue them bread for the nourish
ment of their soules, wherof his holines
being aduertised he presently reuoked his
former prohibition, referring all to the dis.
position of the Generall of the Freers Mi
nors.

Of the feruour of Sainte Clare in her prayer.

CHAP, XXX.

THe principall prayer which God requi
reth of vs consisteth in deuotion for he is
not delighted in the multiplicity of
words but in the feruour of the spirit, the
prayer of the heart is more pleasing vnto him
then that of the mouth the eye on the booke
but the heart with God: this saying is con
formable to that of our Redeemer: when you
pray doe not speake much as the heathens doe:
for they thinke to be heard for the multiplici
tie of their words, but enter into your chamber
in secret: to giue vs to vnderstand that our
prayers are not heard for the multiplying of
words, but the attention and the interiour affe
ction, according to this vsuall saying, not the

voyce

voyce, but the viewe not the harmonie of the
musicke but the heart not the clamour but the
loue doth found in the eares of God: I had rather fayth the Doctour of the Gentiles speake
fiue words with my spirit then ten thousand
with my toung , our Saviour perseuered a
whole hower in prayer in the garden vsing but
few words in like sort the theese made his pe
tition on the crosse, Dauid with one *Peccaui* the
Publican with few words. Our Seraphicall
Father perseuered a whole night with this
sentence, who art thou my God , and who am
I ; often repeating it with great effusion of
teares, and was in such sort absorbed in the
consideration of the diuine greatnes , and his
owne litlenes, that Brother Leo his Confessour
saw him often times eleuated farre from the
ground S. *Clare* his most humble daughter was
so transported in her prayer and absorbed in
the depth of the loue of her Creatour that she
forgot her selfe and her corporall necessities
whereunto she was subiect : the beginning of
the night she reposed a litle , but presenly ari
sing she passed the residue of the time in a pro
found silence, of mentall prayer and holy contemplation and the sweet embracements of her
Spouse her conuersation in spirit being continually aloft with the B. Citizens of heauen:
prayer was the continuall refreshment of her
labours, and assured bulwarke against temptations , and a soueraine remedie in all her necessities : she had full confidence to obtaine

all

all things of the diuine goodnes by the meanes
of prayer: and was accustomed to say, that
euery Christian ought to begg of God in this
life the gift of prayer, sith without it wee can
neither aduance nor persist in spirituall life and
to giue example to her Religious, she made to
appeare in all her actions that her spirit was
allwayes eleuated in God by prayer, the abundance of her teares and the frequent sighes
which proceeded from her heart, the serenity
of her countenance & her eyes fixed on heaué,
did giue assured testimonie of her intense feruour and inflamed deuotion in prayer, to behold her was sufficient to excite others to
deuotion, her countenance was so sweet and
attractiue, and by many externall signes did
manifestly appeare what a cháge and mutation
was wrought in her by the feruour of her
prayer: One day the flame of diuine loue hidden in her soule did exteriourly appeare: for one
of her first disciples by name Sister *Benauenta*
of *Perugia* did see her enuironed with a great
light darting forth such beames of glory as if
she had bene inuested with heauenly beatitude
an other time as on a sunday they sung the An-
tiphone *Vidi aquam egredientem*, being wholy
inflamed in the contemplation of so great a misterie giuing of holy water to her Religious
she cryed out, O daughters call to mind the
most sacred water flowing from the side of our
Redeemer the day of his most dolorous passion, when S. *Clare* came from prayer her face

was

was shining dazeling the eyes of the beholders, and by her words it was easily perceaued
that she came from prayer, discoursing with
such feruour of spirit inflaming the hearts of
the Religious that heard her, procuring heerby an insatiable thirst after celestiall comforts;
in this manner she ordinarily liued replenished
with the knowledge of high secrets, passing
ouer this deceiptfull world in company of her
heauenly spouse *Christ Iesus*, and standing on
this turning wheele she was sustained with
firme constancie perseuering in this eleuation
of soule to the height of heauen, participating
of the diuine secrets which she disclosed to
none if it were not very needful; for she knew
very well that often times an inestimable treasure is lost for a base price of vaine glory: offen-
ding the giuer, and falling into hazard neuer to
enioymore. For the true touch-stone and sol-
lid signe of an humble soule is not to vaunt of
illuminations or to boast that our Lord hath
reuealed this or that vnto them; visions though
neuer so true are often dangerous; but espe-
cially to women who are addicted to vanity:
sometimes it happeneth that in the beginning
they haue true and great fauours, but cursed Satan doth often transforme himselfe into the
shape of an Angell of light according to the
saying of the Apostle, and when he perceaueth **2.Cor.11**
that wee make account of visions he causeth
false to slide in with the true, and if not bad at
least indiscreet which doe corrupt the person

Z   and

and getting footing in the spirits of the too
credulous causeth great disorder: the true signe
and token of heauenly fauours, and the cheese
secret of a spirituall soule, is sanctity of life in
those who receaue such heauenly graces, with
a profound humility proportionable to the su-
blimitie wherunto our Lord doth raise them
neuer abandoning the center of their owne
nothing, and allso Obedience and totall resig-
nation to the will of their Superiour and directour, holding his voice for the voyce of God,
and his aduise for the touch stone to discouer
the verity of apparitions it is the best vision of
all to obay God by the mouth of our guide and
directour which doth neuer deceaue any wher-
as the other are dangerous, these are the true
Oracles and secure lights wherby wee may order our liues, S. *Clare* did neuer relate any vision or apparition but concealed all in the sacred clossett of her heart, and the more God fauored her with his holy visitations the more
she became humble and full of confusion not
reputeing her selfe more virtuous then others.
This sainte was accustomed to call vp the yong
Religious a little before mattins, and to awaken
them with the ordinary signe, to excite them
very often to prayse their Creatour. She lighted the lamp and rung to mattins so that negli-
gence found no entrance into her monastery
nor sloath had there any place: she also by the
sting of sharp reprehension and of her liuely
and effectuall examples expelled tepidity and

                                   irksom-

irkſomnes in prayer and the ſeruice of
God.

How great account Pope Gregorie the ninth made of the prayers of S. Clare, and of a letter to this effect.

CHAP. XXXI.

POpe Gregorie the ninth who before his
promotion to this ſupreame dignitie was
called Cardinall Vgolin Bishop of Oſtie
protectour of the order of *S. Francis* and *S.
Clare,* (he dyed with the reputation of a great
ſaint God ſealing his life with many miracles,)
had a ſinguler confidence in the prayers of this
ſeruant of God haueing experienced their great
vertue and efficacy: and often times when he
was in any difficulty both whiles he was Cardinall and Bishop of Hoſtia and afterwardes
when he was Pope he would by letters re
commend him ſelfe to this holy Virgin de
maůding of her help & ayd knowing aſſuredly
of what importance her aſſiſtance was: this
being in him not onely a great humility but alſo
worthy to be diligently imitated to ſee the Vicar of *Iesus Christ* vpon earth to begg help of a
ſeruant of God; this great Paſtour knew very

well what diuine loue could doe, and how freely pure virgins doe find the port of the confiftorie of the diuine maiefty open. There is extant a very deuout letter written to S. *Clare* by this Pope while he was Cardinall which is heer inferted to make it appeer how the fpirit of God made his refidence in this Prelate and what deuotion he carryed to the fanctity of the glorious virgin S. *Clare.*

To his moft deer fifter in *Iefus Chrift* and mother of his faluation Sifter Clare, Vgoline a miferable finner Bishop of Hoftia, recommendeth him felfe whatfoeuer he is and whatfoeuer he may be, wellbeloued Sifter in *Chrift Iefus*; fince the neceffity of my returne hath feparated me from your holy fpeeches, and depriued me of that pleafure to conferre with you of celeftiall treafures, I haue had much forrow of heart, abundance of teares in my eyes, and haue felt an exceeding greefe: and that in fuch fort that if I had not found at the feet of our Lord *Iefus Chrift* the confolation of his ordinarie piety, I feare I had fallen into fuch anguishes as my fpirit would haue forfaken me and my foule vtterly melted away, and not without reafon, becaufe, that ioye fayled me with which I difcourfed with your good company of the facred bodye of our fweet Redeemer *Chrift Iefus* and of his prefence vpon earth, celebrateing the feaft of Eafter with you and the other feruants of our Lord. And as our B. Sauiour whiles by his dolorous paf-

fion

sion and death he was absent frō the presence
of his disciples they were possessed with an ex-
trem grief and affliction so doth your absence
procure my desolation. And though I acknowledge my selfe a great sinner considering the
prerogatiue of your merits and the rigour of
your most holy Religion, yet without doubt
the multitude of my sinnes is such and so gree-
nously haue I offēded God the vniuersall Lord
that I am not worthy to be vnited to the glory
of the elect; nor to be sequestred from worldly
occupations if your teares and prayers doe not
obtaine me pardon of my sinnes: and therfore
to you I commit my soule, to you I commend
my spirit, as *Iesus Christ* vpon the crosse recommended his spirit to his heauenly Father, to
the end that in the terrible day of the vniuersall iudgment, you giue an account for me if
you be not diligent and carefull of my saluation
for I confidently beleeue that you may obtaine
of the soueraigne iudge whatsoeuer by your
deuotion and teares you shall at any time aske
or demand of him. The Pope speaketh not of
comming to *Assisium* as I desire but I purpose
to come visit you and your Sisters at my first
commodity recommend me I pray you to *Agnes*
your Sister and mine, and to all your other Sisters in *Christ Iesus.*

How Sainte Clare *tormented the diuells*
by prayers.

CHAP. XXXII.

PRayer offred vnto God with humility sub
mission and knowledge of ones selfe, tormenteth and surmounteth the diuells; for
he hauing beene cast into the infernall depthes
by his pride is not able to support the humility of him who singeth the prayses of God
and resigneth himselfe to his will, reputing
himselfe a sinner and defectiue. But often hath
beene forced to confesse himselfe surmounted
tyed and burned by their prayers. This noble
Damsell *Clare* vsed prayer as a shield wherwith
she surmounted the diuell and triumphed ouer
his temptations, beating backe the darts of the
enemie, and burned them exceedingly, a very
deuout woman of the Bishoppricke of *Pisa*
came one day to the monasterie of S. *Damian*
to thanke God and his seruant S. *Clare* for hauing bene by her merits deliuered of fiue diuells that possessed her which going out of her
body confessed that the prayers of S. *Clare* did
exceedingly burne them. Wherat S. *Clare* humbly cast her selfe prostrate in prayer reputing
her selfe vnworthy of the familiarity with so
great a maiesty, conforming her selfe to her

Chron. p.
1. l. 8. c.
15. Luc.
Wad. ad
annum,
1251.
parag. 17

Re-

Redeemer who the night of his passion praying in the garden was not content to bend his knees but cast himselfe on the ground, as she lay with her face on the ground bathed in tears and sweetly kissing it with such content as if she had held in her armes her spouse *Christ Iesus* at whose sacred feet her teares did streame, and her kisses were impressed in the dead of the night; the Prince of darknes swelling with rage and furie to behold so great humility sent one of his most accursed & wickedest spirits to persecute her. He appeared vnto her in the shape of a black a moore, and bid her cease weeping least she did loose her sight, & that she might doe more seruice vnto God in gouerning well her monasterie, thē in weeping so forlornly: the S. perceauing this instigation of Satan, answered him, if I become blind and be not able to gouuerne the Conuent there wil be enow found to doe it who will doe it better then I : thou and thy adherents are truly blind because you can neuer see the incōprehensible light: wherat the diuel fled away confounded. This same night this humble virgin being in prayer after mattins, powring forth riuers of teares in her deuotions, behold the temptour approched appearing in hideous shape like a black boy and sayd vnto her weepe not so much vnlesse thou wilt haue thy braines to dissolue and liquify and purge it at thy eyes and nostrils and become deformed: the inuincible virgin answered him with great feruour. spit-

ting

ting in the face of this Infernall monster: he who serueth *Iesus Christ* cā haue no deformity, these wordes made the furious dragon to burst who presently disappeared and was swallowed in to hel. Being one day after None retired and her minde fixed on God in prayer and her thoughts ingulfed in the Ocean of the diuine goodnes, the cursed diuel came vnto her and beating her very outragiously so farre as to wound her on the face wherby one of her eyes remained all bloudy and a scarre vpon her cheeke crying and howling out in this manner accursed thou doest burne vs by thy prayers, but notwithstanding all these reproches she desisted not from prayer.

Of the great deuotion of saint Francis & sainte Clare to the Natiuitie of our Redeemer and of two notable miracles.

CHAP. XXXIII.

THE B. seruant of God *Francis* and his virtuous daughter *Clare* did beare singular deuotiō to the natiuity of our Redeemer *Christ Iesus*, wherby so high a maiesty had annihilated him selfe assumeing our litlenes and humane nature, bereauing himselfe of

his

his diuine greatnes. This zelatour of the diuine
honour resideing neere to the Citty of Crecio,
resolued to celebrate the festiuity after a new
manner to excite and awake the deuotion of
the faithfull hauing for this effect obtained licence of the Pope to auoyd scandall; he made
to be adorned a great stable with an open Porch
where he caused hay to be layed and a crib: the
he caused an Ox and an Asse to be brought &
assembled together so many Religious me that
they were in number more the the inhabitants
of the place. But for that he had published this
solemnity all the neighbouring people flocked
thither, bringing trumpetts cornets and all
kind of musicall instruments, in such sort as the
montaignes adiacent resounded with harmonie; they ceased not all the night to sing and
make Iubilie in that stable, were *S. Francis* and
a great number of his Religious prayed before
three Images of wood representing the child
Iesus, the glorious virgin Mary and B. *S. Io-*
seph, and ther were lighted great store of wax
tapers which were decently and artificially
placed. The Patriarcke of the poore sung the
ghospell at the midnight masse, and then prea-
ched to the people with such tendernes and
deuotion that being to pronounce *Iesus*, he
was not able but called him the little child of
Bethlem. This feast did not passe without fruit
for a gentleman of a singular note and virtue
called *Iohn de Grecio* a familiar frind of the saint
& imitatour of his virtues, often auouched that

he had seene that night a beautifull child repo-
sing in the Cribb or manger whom S. *Francis*
taking and holding in his Armes sweetly hug-
ged and embraced , the hay being taken away
cured many personnes and beastes of their infirmities, wherby wee may gather that God did
in a singular manner secōd the deuotion of this
his seruant. After the death of the Seraphicall
Father in the place of this stable was built a
magnificent Chappell and in the place of the
manger an Altar was erected to the honour of
God our Creatour. His beloued daughter *Clare*
receaued the same grace and fauour , for one
Christmasse night when both men and Angels
solemnised the festiuitie of the Natiuitie of
our Redeemer all the Religious woemen went
to the quier to mattins leauing their holy mother accompanyed only with her greeuous infirmity , wherfore hauing begunne to meditate
vpon the great misterie of that night ; and lamenting exceedingly that she could not assist
at the diuine seruice she sighing sayd. O my
God thou seest how I remaine heere alone, and
ending this she beganne to heare the mattins
that were sung in the Church of S. *Francis* in
A *ßisium* , very distinctly vnderstanding the
voyce of the Religious , and the very sound of
the Organs , yet was she not so neer the sayd
Church as she might humainly heare what
was sung there but it must necessarily be concluded that this was miraculously done in one
of these two sorts , either that the singing of

of

the fayd Religious was by the will of God ca-
ryed to S. *Clare* or her hearing was extended
by efpeciall grace of God euen to the monafterie of the fayd Religious, this fainte was
moreouer fauored with a heauenly vifion
which did exceedingly comfort and reioyce
her: for she was by allmighty God efteemed
worthy to fee in fpirit his holy Cribb. The
morning following the Religious comming
to vifit her she fayd vnto them, deare Sifters
bleffed for euer be our Lord *Iefus Chrift* that
it hath pleafed him not to leaue me alone as
you haue done, but know that by the grace
of his diuine Maiefty I haue heard all the
feruice that this night hath bene performed
in the Church of our holy Father *Saint
Francis* : recounting vnto them in Order
all which had paffed and as they admired the
Sainte did affure them how the litle child Ie-
fus appeared vnto her at the very hower of
his birth : thus she being abfent merited to
fee what her daughters could not being prefent.

The deuotion of Sainte Clare *to the holy sacra-
ment.*

CHAP. XXXIV.

Clare the true Espouse of *Christ Iesus* exhorted her Religious to beare all honour reuerence and respect to the most
holy Sacrament of the Altar, and often to refe-
ctionate their soules with this diuine repast
and to giue them a paterne and example she receaued her God with so great feruour and deuotion that she rauished the hearts of her
daughters: before she presented her self thervnto a riuer of teares flowed from her eyes
She aproched thervnto with great feare and
humility reuerencing and adoring her Lord &
Creatour hidden vnder these Sacramentall
formes, after the reception she was so absorbed
in the consideration of so great a charity in the
sonne of God that she remained a long time in
extasie without motion: she often sayd to her
Religious: O wonderfull depth of the diuine
Abisse, O most profound humility of the
sonne of God the maister and Lord of the v-
niuersall world to humble himselfe so low as
to giue himselfe vnto vs vnder the forme of

bread

bread, let vs duely ponder my deare Sisters this vnspeakable humility, and purify your hearts before the sacred comunion: be pure and cleane from sinne to the end he may receaue you as he giueth himselfe vnto you. S. *Clare* tooke great comfort to see Churches and Altars well adorned and neatly kept and the ornaments therof decent and that the seruice of God should be performed with deuotion and punctuality, and that nothing requisit should be wanting and though she was very sickly neuertheles she caused her selfe to be set vp in her bedd and stayed her selfe against something in such sort as she might conueniently spinne an exercise which she exceedingly affected and imployed her selfe therin most willingly doing it very delicatly and with the thred of her labour she caused pure fine cloth to be made which she made into Corporalls for the vse of the challice, she once made fiftie cupple of Corporalls and folding them in silke sent them to seuerall Churches in the Valley of *Spoletum.*

How the Mores were driuen from the monasterie and the City of Assisium by
the virtue of the holy Sacrament of the Altar and
by the prayer of S.
Clare.

CHAP. XXXV.

PRayer is a generall instrumēt wherby wee
vndertake and operate all things, and as in
the affaires of this world mooney hath
bene inuented for the facility of commerce, a
meanes so fitt and proper that whosoeuer hath
riches may truly vaunt that he hath all things:
euen so prayer is like a spirituall Coine wherby wee obtaine all things, for she is so powerfull that she can doe all, and swayeth all: she
openeth prisons and setteth Captiues at liberty, she shutteth vp the gates of Hell; and openeth the gates of heauen, she penetrateth the
cloudes and reacheth to God himselfe, she surmounteth all enemies visible and inuisible, in
such sort as the iust man hath more power in
praying then a great Armie in fighting: which
may be prooued by sacred and profane Hi-
storie: but two of *Sainte Clare* shall suffice
vs. The Emperour Frederick the second an

Enemy

Enemy to the Church who hath done so great
mischeeues to Catholickes, wasting destroy-
ing killing and massacring without mercy all he encountred particularly in the valley
of *Spoletum* because it was subiect to the Bishop
of *Rome*, drunk of the vessel of wrath, his Captaines and souldiers being scattered ouer the
feildes as grasse-hoppers with sword to mur-
ther people, & with fier to burne their houses,
the earth was bathed with bloud and furie.
The impyetie of this Emperour did so augment that he had assembled all the Mores that
dwelt vpon the mountaignes and amidst the
desarts to make him selfe the more fearefull to
his vassalls; and after he had by large promises
gained these mores and disposed of them in diuers places, he gaue them at length for retire a
very ancient but ruinated City which to this
present day is called. *Noura des Moros* which
they fortifyed and then retired thither about
twenty thousand fighting men who did much
mischiefe ouer all *Apulia* and in many other
Christian places; One day these merciles
b'oudsuckers thirsting after the bloud of
Christians came vnexpectedly to the City of
A*βisium*, cruelly massacring all they mett,
in fine they went about to blow vp the gates of
the monasterie of S. *Damian* and to scale the
walls wherat the Religious were so surprised
with feare and terrour hearing these inraged
doggs to howle and barke so neer them not
knowing where to seeke for help nor from

whom

whom to hope for deliuery from so eminent
perill but onely by the merrits of their holy
mother whome with infinit teares and sighes
they aduertised of what they heard and
saw. This holy Virgin though very sicke en-
couraged her Religious and made her selfe to
be carryed with incredible constancie to the
gate of the monastery at the entry wherof in
the vewe of all her aduersaries she caused to be
placed very reuerendly the holy sacrament of
the Eucharist in the Pix : before the which
falling prostrate on the ground, she sent forth
from her heart these sweet lamentations, replenished with confidence in her beloued spouse
Christ Iesus; is it possible my God thy will
should be that these thy seruants who can not
vse material weapons to defend them selues &
whome I haue heer brought vp and noursed in
thy holy loue, should now be deliuered in to
the power of the infidell Mores, O my God
preserue them if thou please and me likewise;
for allbeit thy diuine maiesty hath committed
them to my gouuernement; it is not in my
power to defend them from so great a perill
sith this protectió can not be but by a worke
of thine omnipotencie, therfore doe I recom-
méd it to thy diuine maiesty, with all the affection that I am able. So soone as this holy virgin had sent this prayer vnto heauen, she heard
a voice so small and delicate as if it had bin of a
sucking child that sayd. I will protect you for
euer. The holy mother did not yet giue ouer

to pro-

to profecute her prayer in this fort, my God I
humbly befeech thee if fo it be thy holy will to
preferue and defend this thy Citie of *Affifium*
which doth nourrish vs for the loue it beareth
to thy diuine maiesty; wherto God anfwered,
this City shall fuffer much, but I will by my
fauour defend it *S. Clare* haueing heard fo gratious newes lifted vp her face bathed with
teares, and comforted her beloued daughters
faying, deer *Sifters* I affure you that no euill
shall befall you only be carefull to haue a firme
faith and confidence in *Iefus Chrift*: the diuine
affiftance made no delay, for the prefumption
and rage of the *Mores* was incontinently cooled
fo that a fudden vnknowne terrour hauing furprifed them they fpeedely retired ouer the
walls falling one vpon another many of them
being hurt and maymed they were forced to a-
bandon the prey which they had gotten in
to their clawes flying rather the vir tue of the
faint then the fword of the enemie. They being
put to flight by the virtue of the holy facrament
and the prayers of *S. Clare*, she commaunded
her Religious not to difclofe the fauour of this
heauenly voice dureing her life to auoyd the
tickling of vaine glory: from this heroicall act
is brought in the cuftome to draw *S. Clare*
with the Pix of the holy facrament, to shew
to pofterity how in virtue of the power of
God hidden vnder the facramentall formes she
deliuered her monaftery and the City of *Affifiu*
frō the cruelt y & inhumanity of the *Barbarias*.

Luc.
wad. ad
annum.
1255.
§. 7.

How the City of Assisium was an other time deliuered by the prayers of sainte Clare.

CHAP. XXXVI.

Chron.
p.1.l.8.
c.14.
Luc.
Wad.ad
annum.
1251.§.
16.

Vpon an other time one of the principall Captaines of the Emperour *Fredericke* called *Vitalus* Auersa a man ambitious & coueting glory: very couragious and a valiant Souldier, he conducted his troupes to besiedge *Assisium*, and hauing inuironed it he proposed to wast and spoile the Country ther about making a totall ruine to the very trees that were hewed downe and then laying his siedge he vttered menaceing and vaunting oathes that he would not stirre thence till he had giuen the City a victorious assault, and this siedge continued so long that the beseidged beganne to loose courradge wanting many things extremly needfull vnto them : *sainte Clare* hauing heard the rumour of this cursed intention shott a dart of loueing affection vnto heauen powring forth a riuer of teares which she interrupted with many sighes and assembling her Religious she discoursed in this sort with them, my deer Sisters you know our necessities

haue

haue euer bin supplyed by the Charity of this
City, so that wee should be very vngratfull
if wee should not according to our ability
assist them in this extreame necessity: then
she commaunded ashes to be brought her,
and all her Religious to discoise their heades
and to giue them example she beganne to couer her bare head with ashes; where in all the
Religious following her she sayd: goe yee to
our Lord *Iesus Christ* your spouse and with the
the greatest humility and feruent prayers you
câ possible demaûd of him the deliuery of the
towne: it can not be expressed with what feruour and teares these deuout virgins incessantly offred their prayers vnto God the space
of one intire day and night demaunding mercy
in the behalf of the sayd City besieged by their
ennemies, these prayers and teares were of
such force and virtue that God sent them the
day following powerfull succour in such sort
that the enemies Camp was defeated, his
troupes put to flight and the Captaine con-
strayned shamefully and in despight of his forces without sound of trumpett to raise his sie-
ge : and was shortly after slaine.

Of the feruent loue of S. Clare *to the passion of* Iesus Christ.

CHAP, XXXVII.

OVr holy Father S. *Francis* being once demaunded by a Superiour of his Order why he did not caule some spirituall lecture to be read vnto him wherby his spirit might be recreated in his infirmity, he answered him with great feruour, my Brother I doe allwayes find so great consolation and loue in the memory of the life death and passion of our Sauiour *Christ* Iesus that if I should liue to the worlds end I should need no other lecture. He exhorted his Religious often to turne ouer this sacred Booke and in comparison of it to make little reckoning of others: it was also the Manuell of his daughter S. *Clare,* for whosoeuer would haue found her might haue sought her in the woundes of *Christ* Iesus there she spent her time busieing her selfe with great content, she had in such sort ingrauen within the bowells of her hart the sacred Passion of our Redeemer that as often as she called it to memory a torrent of teares streamed frō her eyes she sucked from the sacred woundes of our sauiour some times resentments of sorrow: other times of ioye and consolation with singuler sweetnes:

and

and the croſſe of *Chriſt Ieſus* which with her
deereſt ſpouſe ſhe carryed in her ſoule the
waight wherof gaue her ſo much the more taſt
of contentment as ſhe felt more griefe. The
great abundance of teares which ſhe ſhead
kept her ſome times out of her ſelfe, and the
internall loue which ſhe had imprinted in her
heart, in a manner continually repreſented vnto
her *Chriſt Ieſus* crucifyed. She ordinarily gaue
example by workes of what ſhe taught her
Religious by wordes for often times admoni-
ſhing and inſtructing any of them in priuate
touching any point of the paſſion before her
diſcourſe was ended a ſhower of teares diſtil-
led from her eyes. Among the howers of the
diuine office which are ſung in the church ſhe
aſſiſted with greater deuotion at the ſixt and
ninth hower, becauſe at the ſixt which is at
the twelfth hower of the day *Ieſus Chriſt* was
nayled to the croſſe and at none which is three
howers after he yeelded vp his ghoſt hauing
ſuffred for vs the ſpace of three howers the
torments of the croſſe therfore the ſorrowfull
virgin was at thoſe howers crucifyed with her
Redeemer. She frequently meditated vpon the
miſterie of the fiue woundes haueing learned
by heart the office of the holy croſſe as our holy Father *S. Francis* compoſed it and taught it
vnto her. She was accuſtomed to weare
next her naked ſkinne a cord with thirteene
knots a ſecret remembrance of the woundes
and dolours of our Sauiour. Vpon holy thurſ-

day in lent, at the hower of the agonie of our
Redeemer when he ſweat water and bloud in
the garden this virgin withdrew her ſelfe in to
her Oraᵗory full of greife, and ſett her ſelfe to
accompany the ſonne of God in his prayer as
if ſhe had corporally beheld him and ſuffred
his impriſonment, his deriſions, iniuries, re
proches, buffetts and ſtripes, his condemnation,
croſſe, and ignominious death, exciteing in
her ſelfe the like griefe: wherfore wounded
with compaſſion ſhe ſat downe vpon a ſtraw
bedd, and all that night and the day following
ſhe remained thus abſorbed in God and ingulfed in a profound contemplatiō her eyes being
opē without motion ſhe ſeemed to hold them
fixed in one place and remained ſo inſenſible
being conioyntly Crucifyed with *leſus*
Chriſt, that a Religious familiar vnto her coming often to ſee if ſhe wanted any thing ſhe
found her allwayes in one manner but vpon
the night of holy ſaturday this deuout Reli
gious came to her deer mother with a candle,
and partly by ſignes, partly by wordes makeing her the beſt ſhe could to vnderſtand the
commaundement that the holy Father *ſaint
Francis* gaue her that ſhe ſhould not lett paſſe
one day without takeing & eating ſome thing:
S. *Clare* as comeing from an other world ſayd
vnto her, what need haue you to light a candle
is it not day? wherto the religious anſwered;
mother the night of holy thurſday is paſt as allſo good Fryday and wee are now in the night

of

of Easter eue; the sainte replyed, my daughter
blessed be this sleep which Almighty God at
length after my long desire hath granted me,
but I admonish and commaund you not to
speake heerof to any creature liueing whiles I
shall liue in this world. It was to conceale and
inwrapp in the sacred silence of a profound
humility this great and heauenly fauour to
burie vnder the ashes the sweet and pleasant
poyson of vaine glory.

How sainte Clare *by the signe of the crosse wrought many mira-cles.*

CHAP, XXXVIII.

OVr souueraine Redeemer *Christ Iesus* re-
compenced well the holy desires and
good workes of his beloued Espouse
Clare for as she was inflamed with an infinit
loue of the misterie of the holy crosse, so by
the virtue and power of the same crosse our
Lord did innoble and honour her with many
miracles, often times making the signe of the
holy crosse vpon the sicke they were instantly
cured, which power was indifferently exten
ded to all sortes of diseases a child of three yea
res of the City of *Spoletum* called Mathew had
by mishap thrust a little stone vp his nose, from

Whence

whence it could not be gotten out so that the child grew in great perill of his life, he was brought to S. *Clare* who makeing the signe of the crosse vpon him immediatly the stone fell out and he was perfectly well. One of her owne Religious called *Benauenta* haueing had for the space of twelue yeares an impostume vnder her Arme which did purge by fiue seueall issues, she made vpon it the wholsome signe of the crosse then takeing of the playster all her old soares were intirely cured. An other Religious woeman called *Aymee* being for more then a yeare space afflicted with the dropsie together with an extreme paine in her sides and burning feuer, S. *Clare* mooued with compassion had recourse to her noble and infallible remeady making vpon her body the holy signe of the crosse in the name of her beloued spouse *Christ Iesus*, and the Religious was perfectly cured. A Religious man called *Stephen* hauing a hot feuer that exceedingly vexed him the holy Father S. *Frrancis* sent him to S. *Clare* to make the signe of the crosse vpon him as one who well knew her virtue and perfection which he exceedingly honoured, *saint Clare* as a daughter of obedience presently made vpon him the signe of the holy crosse then left him a little to sleep in the Church in the place where she was accustomed to pray, and he haueing a little reposed arose sound secure and freed of his infirmity. An other seruant of God natiue of Perugia had for two yeares

together

together so lost her voyce that one could scarcely hear her speake, but hauing vnderstood by a vision which she had the night ofthe Assumption of our B. Lady that S. *Clare* should cure her the poor afflicted creature hauing very impatiently expected the breake of the day and then with a strong confidence repaired to the holy virgin and by signes craued her holy benediction which fauour hauing obtained her voyce which so long time she had lost became as cleer and shril as euer it had bin-an other of her Religious called *Christiana* that had a long time bin deafe and hauing in vaine tryed many remedies *S. Clare* hauing made the signe of the crosse vpon her head and touched her eare with her hand she recouuered her hearing as perfect and cleer as euer. An other of her Religious called *Andrea* had a disease in her throat the griefe wherof procured her much impatience, she feeling her selfe one night tormented with her infirmity more then accustomed afflicted and impatient that her paine did rather increase then diminish, she so crushed and pressed her throat making therby appeer her intention to choake her selfe thinking heerby to expell that swelling , and through ignorance attempting to doe more then was the will of God: but whiles that poor Religious busied her selfe in that folly S. *Clare* by diuine inspiration had knowledge therof; and calling one of her Religious she sayd vnto her goe downe speedely to the cooke and cause her to boyle an egge and

then

then cause Sister Andrea to swallow it which
done bring her to me , the Religious instantly
accomplished her commaundment and forth-
with brought the egg to the sicke party
whome she found little better then dead hauing so crushed her throat that she could not
speake, yet she made her swallow the egg as
well as she could then raising her vp from her
straw bed she with much labour lead her to
S. *Clare*. who spake vnto her in this manner,
wretched Sister confesse thee to God and haue
contrition for what thou intededst to doe, and
acknowledge that *Iesus Christ* will giue thee
health much better then thou with thine owne
handes hadst proposed to doe , change this
euill life in to a better for thou shalt neuer recouuer an other sicknes that shall succeed this
but shalt dye therof; these wordes procured in
this Religious the spiritt of compunction and
contrition so that she being intirly cured of this
greeuous infirmity she ameded her life: a little
after an other sicknes tooke hold of her as S.
Clare had fortold wherof she piously ended her
life. It doth manifestly appeer by these examples and many other maruelous things which
this holy virgin wrought in virtue of this
wholsome signe that the tree of the crosse of
our B. sauiour *Iesus Christ* was deeply planted
in her hart and that in an admirable manner the
fruites therof did interiourly recreat her soule sith the leaues did worke exteriously such
remeadies by the hands and merrits of this
glorious Lady.   *How*

*How sainte Clare besought her su-
periours that she might enioye the
presence of her sister whome
she beholdeth three times
crowned by an
Angell.*

CHAP. XL.

Saint *Francis* well knowing that S. *Agnes*
was adorned & imbellishd with all sort of
perfection sent her to *Florence*, to found a
new monasterie called *Mont Celi*, wherofshe
made her Abbesse; this holy virgin wonne many soules to abandon the world and serue *Christ
Iesus* by her holy conuersation exemplar life &
virtuous discourses and as a true contemner of
worldly things and imitatour of our Redeemer she planted in this monasterie and in many
others (conformable to the intention of our
holy Father S. *Francis*) the Euangelicall pouerty. S. *Clare* seeing her self assaulted with ma
ny infirmities and to draw neer her end desired
greatly the company of her Sister *Agnes* the
small time she was to remaine in this life wher-
vnto superiours condescended. Wherfore B.
Agnes hauing left her monastery of Florence

Cc 2   well

well founded in Religiō and sanctity and Sister *Clare Vhaldini* a most vertuous Religious to succeed her, she returned to the monastery of S. *Damian* to the exceeding great spirituall cōsolation of her Sister. The prudent mother being one night in prayer saw her Sister *agnes* raysed from the ground and an Angell who at three seuerall times crowned her with three seuerall garlands or crownes, the day insuing she inquired of her what prayer or contemplation she had made the night past, *Agnes* through humility was vnwilling to discouuer her meditation, but being vrged ther vnto by obedience she sayd vnto her, I did consider the great bounty and clemency of Almighty God wherwith he doth support so many sinners which did excite in me an excessiue sorrow, next I did ponder the infinit loue of Iesus Christ to mankind vndergoeing death to saue him: thirdly I did consider with griefe, and compassionate the poor soules in purgatory by reason of their vnspeakable torments, and for that they can not help them selues I did in their behalfe require mercy of the sacred woundes of our Redeemer.

Of the admirable constancie of sainte Clare *in her* sicknes.

CHAP. XLI.

IF wee could well vnderstand and conceaue what good and profitt wee reape by afflictions and infirmity wee would embrace them with great affection and content, and would conserue them as pearles Iewells and pretious stones; they are the porters of heauen the forrunners of cōsolatiō, the fauours of heauē, the guides of our life, & the cure & remedie of all our miseries: aduersitie doth serue vs in such sort as the hammer doth the gold smith to forge and frame his crowne, the fier doth burne the gold whiles it is in the furnace but therby it is purifyed refined and beautifyed: behold the tryall of a iust man who being cast in to the fyer of tribulation cometh forth in his thoughts more humble, in his prayers more deuout, in his conscience more pure and neat: and more constant & perseuerant in the exercise of virtue and patience, in this furnace God our Creatour would make tryall of the generositie of his beloued daughter *Clare*, for in her life time she was oppressed with sundry great maladies, but principally the space of 28. yeares, resting continually on her straw bed; remaining invincible vnder the waight of her infirmities, with a ioyefull countenance and setled trai quillity acccompanyed with a meeke serenity no impatient word euer escapeing her mouth, but rather according to the example of her Seraphicall Father who amidst his agonie sung most heauenly ditties, and vttered most holy wordes and Iaculatory prayers which though but breife were notwithstanding efficacions cordiall and penetrating and knocking at the heart of God, and returning back loaden with consolation, he felt lesse irckfomenes in his afflictions: she neuer sought to be freed or solaced in her paines and tribulations but that she might he faithful to her Creatour begging allways that her courage might be as great as her infirmity confideing allways that these momentary torments would soone begett eternity and incomparable glory, by this patience produceing the fruits of virtues which were ripened by aduersitie and sufferance.

How the Cardinall Protectour of the Order visited S. Clare in her suknes.

CHAP. XLII.

S*ainte Clare* had most inuincibly and infatigably runne in the race of the most high Pouerty the space of forty yeares hauing broken the Alabaster of her bodye by austeare fastes disciplins and mortification, by this meanes filling the holy Church with the sweet Odour of her virtues, wherby she drew after her an infinit number of soules to the seruice of *Christ Iesus*, now rūning on swiftly through the course of many infirmities her corporall forces being alltogether extenuated and in a māner exhausted she seemed euery moment to draw neer her end but God intēded to honour her before her death with the presence of his Holines and the most notable Prelates of the Roman Church whose peculiar daughter she was: before all from the Citty of Perusia hastened in great diligence Reginald Cardinall of Ostia (who was afterwardes installed in the high throne of S. *Peter*, and called Allexander the fourth) protectour of the Order, by Office her Father, and by particular solicitude her

gouuer-

gouernour fosterer and friend in most pure and
chast amitie to visit and comfort her; she be
sought him with all submission to administer
vnto her the most B. sacramēt of the Eucharist
who haueing condescended to her deuotion
she was replenished with ioye, and her heart
like to haue flowen into an eternall extasie,
haueing receaued him whom she cherrished
a thousand times more then her owne life,
darting forth words so inflamed with the loue
of God, that all there present dissolued in to
teares. Then the worthy Prelate propounded
an exhortation to the Religious woemen. S.
Clare besought him with great humility and in
the name of our Redeemer Christ Iesus, to take
into his protection that her Familie and all
other poor Sisters of her Order. But principally she besought him with abundance of
teares to obtaine of the Pope & the Colleadge
of Cardinalls the confirmation of the priui
leadge of holy pouerty assureing him that she
should dye with exceeding content if she
might receaue that fauour before her departure: which the Cardinall did promise her and
did execute as a faithfull protectour of her Religion, for being come to Perusia he declared
to the supreame Pastour the indisposition of
his daughter and her most pious request: the
Vicar of Iesus Christ granted all, and gaue vnto
him licence by Apostolicall authority to confirme the desire of the virgin as appeereth by
the letters patents the which he presently sent

vnto

vnto her. It is in this manner: Reginald by the the grace of God Bishopp of Hoſtia and of Veletre to his moſt deer mother and daughter in *Ieſus Chriſt Clare*, *Abbeſſe* of *ſaint Damians* at *Aſiſium* and to her Religious both preſent and to come, health and Fatherly benediction for ſo much as you my deer daughters in *Chriſt Ieſus* contemning the pompes and delights of the world, and following the Footſteps of *Ieſus Chriſt* and his holy mother haue choſen to be Corporally incloſed to ſerue God, wee prayſeing your holy reſolution will with our Fatherly affection curteouſly graunt vnto you your deſire and holy requeſts, and therfore inclineing to your pious ſupplications wee confirme by the Popes authority and ours for you and all thoſe that ſhall ſucceed you in your monaſterie the forme and Rule of life by the meanes of a holy vnion, and of the moſt high and ſublime Pouerty: which the holy Father *ſaint Francis* hath giuen you to obſerue both by word and by writing.

*How Pope Innocent the fourth visited
saint Clare before her death
and of a notable mira-
cle done in his presence.*

CHAP. XLIII.

THis generous seruant of *Christ Iesus* being
more assaulted with sicknes then accustomed, a sword of sorrow pierced the
hearts of her daughters in such sort
as they dissolued into teares sighing and
lamenting fearing euery moment to be depriued of her most gratefall presence: but God
had otherwise disposed as it was declared by
vision to a very deuout Religious woman of
the monastery of *Saint Paule* of the Order of
S. Benedict, it seemed vnto her that she and all
her Religious Sisters did visit the holy mother
Clare at the Conuent of *S. Damian* who lay in
a rich and magnificent bed about which they
stood all weeping and lamenting expecting her
death: and that in the meane time there drew
neer to her beds-head a most beautifull woeman, who sayd vnto them, my daughters weep
not for her who shall yet liue: for she can not
dye vntill our Lord with all his disciples doe
arriue, the successe hath declared the truth of

the

the oracle for towardes the latter end of the
yeare 1252. Pope Innocēt the fourth represent
ing *Iesus Chrijt* vpon earth in his millitant
Church, and the Lords Cardinalls representing
the disciples of our Redeemer did expressly
depart from Perusia and came to *Aſsiſium* to
visit this holy damsell, the supreame Bishop
not doubting but she whose life he had already
approued was the most perfect in sanctity of
all woemen in her time and by consequence
worthy to haue her death honored with his pre
sence: being entred with fower Cardinalls and
fower Freer Minours disciples of the Seraphicall Father in to the chamber where this Celestiall Doue did repose, coming to her bed he
gaue her his hand to kiſse she receaued this fauour with great content, and besought him
with all reuerence she might allso haue the fauour to kiſse his Apoſtolicall Feet, the Pope to
satisfy her deuotion satt downe vpon a little
bench and then presented her his Feet vpon
which this holy Saint reuerently layed her
face and her mouth most affectionatly kiſseing
them: then with an Angelicall serenity she de
maunded of him remiſsion of all her sinnes, the
Pope answered: I would to God my daughter
that I needed no greater pardon when I shall
come to dye : in fine he gaue vnto her the benefit of absolution, and his benediction : his
holines hauing a long time conferred with
S. *Clare* hearing from her mouth as from the
secretary of the holy ghost heauenly and diuine

doctrine

doctrine, bread was brought both for her refection and for all the Religious, she besought the Pope to blesse the bread, the soueraigne Bishop sayd vnto her; my daughter *Clare* I will haue you to blesse it your selfe makeing thervpon the signe of the holy crosse; the saint replyed, holy Father pardon me if you please: for if I shall doe it I should be worthy of reprehension, presuming to giue a blessing in the presence of your holynes, wher to he answered well my daughter that no presumption be imputed vnto you but that you may merrit by it, I commaund you by holy obedience to blesse these loaues makeing vpon them the signe of the holy crosse she blushed exceedingly to see her selfe commanded by the vicar of Christ in presence of the Cardinalls whose eyes were all fixed vpon her admireing her rare modestie: but considering she was compelled after she had eleuated her eyes and hart to heauen to inuocate the holy ghost as an obedient daughter she lifted vp her hand and blessed them: it was admirable for the crosse remained imprinted vpon euery one of these loaues, and the loafe which the saint was to eat brake and deuided it selfe in to fower peeces in forme of a crosse: part of that bread was eaten through deuotion and the rest conserued for reliques, and the Pope remained much amazed and gaue thankes to God; her minde being not yet satisfyed with the letters pattents giuen by Apostolicall authority by the protectour

of the

of the Order concerning the priuileadge of pouerty she besought his holines in all humility and submission to graunt her an expresse Bull which he promised her; but afterwards perceauing this fauour to be deferred (for the soueraigne Bishop thought allwayes to induce *Saint Clare* not to bind her Religious to such an extreame pouerty) fearing that after her death all would be buried in obliuion a little before her departure she sent a man expresse to the holy sea Apostolick beseeching him to confirme her demand, the Pope seeing her perseuerance and last will granted her request the tenth yeare of his Popedome according to the pattents specifyed in the 21. Chapter which were deliuered vnto her three dayes before her death which she receaued and kissed them with great ioye for as a true louer of pouery she languished after this fauour. The Vicar of *Iesus Christ* being departed, and hauing receaued the same morning the sacred communion, at the handes of the Reuerend Father Prouinciall: the diuine clemencie did yet further augment her consolation for the virtuous Religious Sister *Francis* did behold a globe of fyer to conuert in to a most beautifull child standing close by the holy virgin, comforting and cherrishing her with vnspeakable sweetnes to reioyce her heart; then with her handes ioyned and her eyes eleuated to heauen; weeping she sayd to her Religious:

my

my daughters prayse and magnify God for the inestimable fauour and benefit which he hath vouchsafed to doe me it being so great that heauen and earth is not able to acknowledge it, for this day I haue receaued God my Creatour and haue merited to see his Vicar vpon earth. The foresayd Sister *Francis* doth depose that she did see vpon the solemnity of the holy Apostles S. *Phillipp* and *Iames* a most glorious and beautifull child who standing vpon the lapp of the sainte held ouer her head twoe shineing and refulgent wings, which some times he raised vpwards other whiles letting them fall downe againe they couuered after an admirable manner the head and shoulders of S. *Clare*.

Sainte Clares *patience in her sicknes. And how she comforted her Sister* Agnes,

CHAP. LXIV.

AFter the aboue mentioned visitations she was wonderfully oppressed with infirmity from the beginning of the month of December vntill the month of August which she indured with such patience and constancie that ther neuer escaped her mouth the least word of

com-

Complaint how violent soeuer her torments were; yea haueing bin seauenteene dayes without being able to take any sustenance which could be presented vnto her she was notwithstanding so fortifyed with diuine grace that she excited and stirred vp all those who visited her to be dilligent in the seruice of God giueing them such fitt instructions as if she had penetrated in to their very harts so directly she hitt the mark and touched their wounds. As her life decayed and drew towardes an end Brother *Renauld* of the Order of *S. Francis* a man of singular perfection spake vnto her certaine deuout wordes animating her to indure courragiously the last assaults, and to beare with patience her greeuous sicknes which did so torment her: she answered him with a smileing countenance and cieere voyce: O my Brother how much am I obliged to my Sauiour and Redeemer *Christ Iesus* for since that by the meanes of his great seruāt *Francis* I haue tasted the bitternes of his dolorous Passion I haue neuer in my whole life found paine which could afflict me, nor euill that could hurt me, nor infirmity how great soeuer that can contristate me, for ther is nothing insupportable to a hart that loueth God and to him that loueth not, all is insupportable: her delight was to speake of God the vanity of the world, death and the recompence of the blessed her Religious stood about ther mother, of whom within a short space they should be orphans,

neither

neither sleep nor the takeing of their other necessities could separate them from her company, for the comfort they tooke in her presence made them forgett all those commodi-
ties, in particular her deer Sister *Agnes* was
wounded with sorrow and greife, being thus
vehemently afflicted she earnestly besought
her Sister Clare not to forsake her but as they
had bin lincked together in loue and affection
so they might not be separated by horrid death
beseeching the diuine maiesty that she might
be deliuered from the bondes of this miserable
bodye. This heauenly doue loueing her as her
owne hart and as the apple of her eye, answered her; my deer Sister whom I loue most cordially since it is the will of God I should depart, remaine you heer ioyfull and weepe not,
for I assure you our Lord will come very soone
to visit you with an vnspeakable consolation
before your death. Which came to passe the 97.
day following: for our Redeemer (as the spouse of the Espouse) appeered vnto her graciously
beholding her and and giueing her a tast of the
eternall Felicity, (according to the prophesie
of her Sister *Clare*) before her death, inuiteing
her to the wedding of the lambe the yeare
1253. the 16. of nouember, 56. of her age,
compleat in all perfection: God hath manifested the glory of her soule by a number of miracles which haue bin wrought at her tombe.

*Of the spirit of Prophecie in sain-
te Clare and how she was
visited by the Religi-
ous of* Florence.

CHAP. XLV.

S Ainte *Clare* was adorned with the spirit of
prophesie which appeared in seueral occa
sions & first the Seraphical Father sending
once fiue noble damsells vnto her to be admitted amongst the number of her disciples, she
addmitting sower refused the fifth by name
called *Casiam Thatholia* who with great in
stancie besought *sainte Clare* to admit her in
like sort but the sainte foretold her she would
proue vnconstant and not perseuer with them,
but the damsell vrgeing the sainte to proceed
more affectionatly and seriously with her affir
meing by oath that she would perseuer among
them wherfore surmounted with her importunity she admitted her but before a yeare was
expired she returned to the world, prouing the
prophesie of S. *Clare* to be true. One Hugoline
Peeter Gicordonis a noble man of A*ssisum* after
he had bin foolish twoe and twentie veares &
parted from his wife *Guiducciam* who was very pious she foretold they should liue againe

E e   very

very peaceably together and be comforted
with a fine child which came to passe according
to her prophesie as the man him selfe testifyed
in the processe of her Canonization. Her Religious kneeling round about her bed powring
forth riuers of teares, for greefe of her departure, she turning towardes them sayd: my
daughters, go meet your Sisters coming frō the
monasterie neer florence to visit me in my last
sicknes goe speedely for they stay at the gate &
haueing refected and refreshed them bring
them in to me *vt benedicat eas anima mea
antequam moriar*; that my soule may blesse
them before I dye; they were receaued by *saint
Clare* with great ioye and consolation and she
gaue vnto them a vayle which she ordinarily
wore which they carryed with them to their
monastery of florence where it is yet kept by
the Religious of the sayd monastery for a Re-
lique, this Conuent hath since bin built and e-
stablished in the City. It is a thing very ordinarily seene that the wordes of dying parents
do take a great impression in the hearts of the
children and are retained as oracles, the glorious virgin & mother *S. Clare* with a smileing
looke and Angelicall countenance gaue vnto
her Religious a thousand heauenly documents
recōmending to her holy Familie al sort of rare
virtues in particular the loue of God and their
neighbour, obedience to superiours, and the
strict and sublime pouerty: she foretold them
what should befall them after her death then

ioyning her handes in forme of a crosse she gaue her holy benediction to all her Religious both present and absent.

The Benediction of S. Clare.

IN the name of the most holy Trinity A-men. My deerly beloued Sisters our Lord giue you his Benediction and behold you with the eye of his mercy giueing you his peace, as also to all those who shall enter and perseuer in our Colledge & monastery & allso into all other monasteries of the Order who shall perseuer vnto the end in the most holy pouerty. I *Clare* seruant of *Iesus Christ* and little plant of our holy Father *S. Frrancis* your mother and Sister allthough vnworthy doe be-seech our Redeemer by the intercession of his most holy mother, of the Archangell *S. Michaell* and the holy Angells, of our holy Father *S. Francis* and all the holy saints, that he will giue and confirme vnto you this Benediction in heauen and in earth, in earth multiplying in you his holy grace; and in heauen exalting you with his saintes: I giue you my benediction whiles I am yet in this life, & after my death,

as much as I am able, and mo re then I am able.
Amen.

How many persons of note and disciples of saint Francis assisted at sainte Clares death.

CHAP. XLVI.

THe deuotion and affection which euery one bore vnto her did dayly increase in such manner as she was honored for a saint, being frequently visited by Cardinalls, Bishopps, and other Prelates, and as God drew neerer vnto her and that her soule was ready to depart, this holy virgin desired that some of the most holiest and spirituallest Freer Minors should assist and be present to discourse vnto her of the passion of our Redeemer; the more to inflame her in his holy loue by their pious exhortations: amongst others Brother Iuniperus disciple to S. *Francis* came fitly to the purpose S. *Clare* loued him singularly for his great sanctity and familiarity with God, (he was called the Archer of Iesus Christ by reason of his wordes so inflamed in diuine loue which penetrated to the harts of the hearers like inflamed darts) he entertained her with such infla-

med

med difcourfes of her Creatour that this good
Lady fild with ioy at the fight of him demāded
if he knew no new thing of God: brother Iunipere anfwered fparkling forth fuch fublime
feruour that she remained fully fatisfyed and
content. Finally turning her Angelicall face
towardes her deerly beloued daughters and
Sifters who ftood there powring forth abūdan-
ce of teares, she recommended vnto them in
this her laft paffadge the moft holy pouerty,
yeelding thankes vnto allmighty God for the
manifold benefits which she had receaued from
his diuine maiefty, relating many in particular,
then she gaue againe her benediction to all the
Religious of her monaftery both prefent and
abfent and to all thofe that should enter in to
her order: there were alfo prefent two companyons of S. *Francis*, Brother Angell comforting the affembly and the moft innocent brother Leo who ceafed not to kiffe the bed of the
damfell ready to abandone this world; her
daughters bewayling at her Feet accompany-
ing her foule vnto heauen with teares and la-
mērations finding no confolation but in defire
to accompany her.

How S. Clare was visited by our Redeemer and his glorious virgin Mother and of her B. departure.

CHAP, XLVII.

Saincte *Clare* the B. Espouse of *Chrift* Iefus being curioufly elaborated and rarely carued and made fitt by the blowes of tribulation, temptation, and infirmity , as a firme and liuing ftone which was to be placed in a principall corner of the celeftiall H*ierufalem* , the cold fweat mounting to her forhead and the painfull gripes and pangs of death knocking at the gate of her heart; fhe heard the fweet voyce of her fouueraigne Redeemer calling her to him felfe , her foule being now euen ready to depart with great tranquillity: fhe fpake moft fweetly to her B. foule faying, goe confidently my foule goe fecurely for thou haft a good guid to conduct thee through this voyage , for he who hath created thee hath fanctifyed, and hath allwayes conferued thee affecting thee with a tender loue equall with that of a mother towards her child , and thou my God be prayfed for hauing created me. Sifter *Anaftafia* asked of her to whome it was fhe fpake: to whome fhe replyed faying I fpeake to my B. foule which hath bene preuented with

the

the benedictions of our Lord: brother *Iunipere* beginning to read the Paſſion of our Redeemer (which was the Manuel of this Virgin) *Chriſt Ieſus* her glorious and triumphant Spouſe appeared vnto her in Royall maieſty refulgent as the ſunne bearing in his aſpect the beauty and ornament of heauen darting forth rayes of diuine glory, he with a ſmileing countenance inuited her to the company of his Eſpouſes. S. *Clare* was ſo tranſported with ioye as it was admirable her heart did not breake therwith and her ſoule take her flight to the heauenly manſions, ſhe diſpoſed her ſelfe thervnto and called her coſſin Siſter *Ayme* and ſayd vnto her my daughter doe you not behold the king of glory whom I ſee, behold there is my beloued ſpouſe who doth inuite me to eternall manſiós and to the Pallace of the immortall wedding, now in the meane while ſhe darted forth inflamed affections towards her beloued, breathing after nothing but to be diſſolued from this body and to be ſett free from this troubleſome captiuity that ſhe might take her flight vnto heauen. Siſter *Benauenta* being tranſperced with a dart of ſorrow caſting her ſight to the chamber doore ſhe ſaw with her corporall eyes to enter in an honorable Proceſſion of Virgins moſt richly cloathed in white garments, euery one wearing on her head a crowne of gold beſett with pearlés and glittering ſtarres, among them was one who ſeemed to be the Empreſſe, ſurpaſſing in maieſty and

m oſt

most magnificently adorned wearing on her
head a most pretious diademe besett with
pearles, Rubies, and a brightnes so resulgent
that it changed the darknes of the night into
cleere day, this was the mother of God queene
and Empresse of heauen, who with a maiesti-
call but smileing countenance went directly to
the pure and innocent virgin *Clare* who lay in
agonie; and embraceing her tenderly she gaue
her the kisse of peace; and to assigne her to ap-
peere personally in glory she brought with her
a Robe or garment of inestimable value which
this souueraigne Ladye gaue vnto this
heauenly damsell that she might adorne her
selfe therwith to meete her heauenly Spouse
according to this saying of *saint John*. The
wedding of the Lamb is come and the time set
downe for the celebratiõ therof, & the Espouse
is cloathed in rich garments white as snow.
Which wee see fulfilled in this happy virgin,
for *Christ Iesus* sent vnto her by the handes of
his sacred mother the ornaments wherin she
was present her selfe at the feast. What ioye &
cõfort did her soule then feele, what heauenly
security what extraordinary iubilie, what spirituall grace what certainty & pledges of eternall glory did she then receaue. Amidst these
sweet embracements she yealded vp her holy,
beautifull, and happy soule into the armes of
her Creatour conuered with Laurells and loaden with Palmes tryumphantly to enter into
the Celestiall Kingdome, seruing her selfe
                                          with

with death as a footstoole to step to eternall felicity, changing her haire-cloath for a stole of immortality, pouerty for euerlasting riches, pennance for perpetual ioy & happines, for her fasting in this exile she is now satiated at the magnificent table of the heauenly inhabitants and for the villity and humility of her garments she is resplendétly reuested with glory, her continuall incessant sighes and desires panting after the presence of her beloued are now fulfilled by the B. Vision of God and by the happy fruition of the souueraigne good; leauing vs an open way wherby the example of her sanctity wee blind and miserable wretches may forsake the breife transitory and deceiptfull pleasures, and may pursue the permanent true and euerlasting.

Of the honorable Obsequies of saint Clare.

CHAP. XLVIII.

Th e soule of *S. Clare* hauing left this mortall life the rumour of her death was presently diuulged ouer all the City o fAßsium, from whence both men and woemen came flocking with great concourse to the monastery in such sort as the City seemed to be

forsaken and left empty, thither came the offi
cers of iustice with great store of armed men
who guarded the monastery that night for feare
least that rich treasure should be taken from
them: the City of *Assisium* delegated certaine
persons of account to his holines in the City
of *Perusium* He residing there both by reason
of Calamities of the Church as allso to expect
the diuine ordination concerning the departure of his daughter *Clare* whom he loued
with a tender and Fatherly affection esteeming
her to be the most holyest damsell of her time,
and desireing to be present at her obsequies haueing heard the newes he departed from Perusia with all his Court and comeing to *Assisium*
the day following he entred into the monastery of S. *Damian* where he contemplated her
dead (whom he had visited in her sicknes)
sheading abundance of teares through deuotion beholding the beautifull face of this heauenly inhabitant, they lifted vp her bodye. and
with torches, wax tapers and boughs with all
reuerence and deuotion they carryed her in to
the Church, where the office was celebrated
by the Cardinalls and Cleargie in the presence
of Pope Innocent the fourth and an incredible
number of Prelates, Abbots, Lords, and persons of quality who flocked thither to exibitt
this last dutie and honour to S. *Clare*, the Can-
tores beginning the office of the dead the Pope
would haue had the office of virgins manifesting a desire to Canonize her before her bodye

was

was interred. But *Arnould* Cardinall of *Hostia* and Protectour of the Order aduised him that notwithstanding that the commaundement of his holines was iust by reason of her singular merrits, yet it was better that that should be done with more deliberation & counsel. The Pope then permitted them to prosecute solemnly the office of the dead according to the custome; the sayd Cardinall of *Hostia* made the Funerall Sermon hauing taken for his theame *Vanitas vanitatum & omnia vanitas*, declareing the vanity of honour riches pleasures and delights of this world highly extolling the wise and noble despiser of all vanities he might very pertinently discourse as eye-witnes of the illustrious actions of this most renowned virgin hauing forcible argumets wherwith to mooue the harts and eyes of his auditours to teares of deuotion by his Oration. The Funeralls being very honorably concluded: the Cittizens of *Assisium* thought it not conuenient that this inestimable Iewell and pretious threasure should be so farre distant from their Citie they caused this holy bodye to be transported with great pompe singing Psalmes and Himnes accompanyed with the harmonie of sundrie musicall instruments and solemne procession carrying it to the Church of *S. George* where the bodie of *S. Francis* had first been layed. It being very conuenient that he who in his life had directed her should also prepare the place of her sepulcher ; there was then a great concourse and

multi-

multitudes of people flocking from sundry
Citties townes and villages about *assisium* to
giue thankes vnto God and to proclaime this
Virgin a glorious sainte who now liueth and
raigneth with God and his Angells, and therfore deserueth to be honored by men vpon
earth. O glorious Ladye pray now for vs and
gaine our soules to God as thou hast drawne
many vnto him liueing in this world. *Sainte
Clare* passed from this life to the next the
yeare of our Lord 1253. the 11. of August
the 42. yeare after her vocation to Religion, and the 60. of her age, she was buried
the 12. vpon which day the Church doth so-
lemnise her festiuitie.

Of the *Canonization* of S. Clare.

CHAP. XLIX.

POpe *Innocent* the fourth hauing beene very familiar with S. *Clare* whiles she liued in this vale of teares, visiting her
in her last sicknes, seene her after her death,
and assisted at her Funeralls, and knowne her
for a Paragon of saints in her time, he much
desired to Canonize her: for this subiect the
28. of october the same yeare 1253. he gaue ex-

preſſe

presse commission to *Bartholmew* Bishop of
Spoletum to examine her life, perfections, and
miracles, who with *Leonard Arch-Deacon* of
Spoletum, *Iames Arch-Priest*, Brother *Leo* heer-
tofore Confessour to the Seraphicall Father
S. *Francis*, Brother Angell of *Rieta* one of the
twelue first disciples of the sayd saint. And
Brother M*arck* Confessour of the Religious
woemen of S. *Damian* did prosecute and perfect the processe by Acts of publicke notaries
and an infinit number of witnesses worthy of
Faith and credit, which they presented to the
vicar of *Iesus Christ* vpon earth, at the begining of the yeare following. But the Pope constrained to take his iourney towardes Naples,
for the pregnant affaires of the Church, loaden with age, labour and persecutions and
full of merits, he was stroken by death, bowing
to the rigour of this cruell Law the 25. of December the yeare 1254. yealding vp his soule
to God and his bodye to the earth in the Conuent of the Freer Minors in the City of Naples, to the great greife and detriment of the
Church. *Reginauld* Cardinall and Bishop of
Hostia, succeeded Innocent the fourth in the
chaire of S. *Peeter*, and was called Allexander the fourth, vnderstading that the renowne
of the saint did dayly augment and that euery
one desired her Canonisation he made choi-
se of persons of great authority, prudence, and
learning, to examine her life and merits, and
being duely informed how this virgin had

Luc.
Wad. ad
annum.
1254.
§.11.

bin irreprehéſible in her actions and a moſt
bright mirrour of virtue and perfection, and
that God had ſealed the eminency of her holy life by an infinit number of true and approued miracles he ordained and ſett downe a
day for her Canoniſation wherat were aſſem-
bled with his holines many Cardinalls Arch.
Biſhops, Biſhops, Prelates and great number
of Prieſtes , and Religious men; with a great
number of Lords knights and gentle men, and
others of lower rack; before whome the Pope
propounded this holy ſubiect , demaunding
therin aduiſe of the Prelates, who with one
accord conſented and. beſought that this Ladie might be Canoniſed in the Church ſith
Ieſus Chriſt had illuſtrated her in heauen . In
this ſort then two yeares after her deceaſe
Pope Alexander did inrole her in the Cata
logue of ſaintes: ordaineing that her feaſt
ſhould be ſolemniſed on the twelft day of
Auguſt , this Canoniſation was celebrated
with all magnificency in the City of *Anagnie*
in the great Church: the yeare 1255. and the
firſt yeare of the Popedome of the ſayd Pope;
to the prayſe and glory of our ſouueraine Creatour and mercifull Redeemer.

Luc.
Wadad.
annum
255. §.
15

*Of the translation of the bodyes of S. Fran-
cis and S. Clare, with other
particulars.*

CHAP. L.

THe glorious Father *S. Francis* a louer of
humility and contempt of himselfe, euer
desired that his bodie after his death
might be buried in the most vile and abiect
place of *Assisium*, he was not frustrated of his
demaund or prophesie, for Pope *Gregorie* the
ninth coming to *Assisium* for the Canonisation
of the sayd saint, the yeare 1228. he caused to
be built a famous temple to his honour laying
himselfe the first stone in the presence of a
great multitude of people, in the most abiect
and contemptible place of the City which was
called the mount of *Hell* where malefactours
were executed, but since it is called the mount
of *Heauen*, contributing towards this building the greatest part of his reuenues in the
valley of *Spoletum* The yeare 1230. the same
Pope caused to be assembled the General Chapter of the Order of Freer Minors in the City
of *Assisium* and caused to be published ouer all
Europe the translation of the bodie of *saint
Francis* from the Church of *S. George* where it

*Luc.
Wad. ad
annum.
1230. §.
1.*

had

had reposed the space of fower yeares to the
new Church built to the honour of the saint,
thether came aboue two thousand Religious
men and faint *Anthonie of Padua* amongit the
reft; and of feoulars of all degrees and qualities
the number was innumerable who reforted
thether from all quarters, in fuch fort as the
City being not able to containe them they
were compelled to retire into the fields vnder
tents and pauillions, they now all expected
with great denotion the arriual of his Holines
according to his promife: he fent his expreffe
Apoftolicall Nunces both to plead his excufe
for that he did not come himfelfe in perfon for
fome law full impedimen's which hindered
him: and to adorne this new Church with a
great croffe of gold inriched with many pretious ftones of ineftimable value wherin there
was inchaffed a great peece of the true croffe;
and allfo many other ornaments and rich vef-
fels to embellish the high Altar, and other rich
donaries, befides a large Almes to detray all
charges and to perfect the worke, the tranfla-
tion was celebrated the 25. of May. The yeare
1230. in moft magnificent Pompe, the holy bodie figned with the feale of our Redemption
was placed in a Chappell vnder ground as it is
declared in the 29 Chapter; this folemnity was
moft illuftrious by many miracles which God
wrought infauour of the faint. But to the end
that the temple of *S. George* wherin this ineftimable Iewell had repofed might euer be in

Luc.
Wad. ad
annum.
1230.
parag.2.

great

great honour the Supreame Bishop by Apoſtolicall authority gaue it to his beloued
daughter *Clare*, ordaining expreſſely for this
end his Procuratour to build a new Church
with a monaſterie thervnto adioyning for the
Religious woemen of *S. Damian* for the greater commodity and ſafety of their perſons this
Conuent was not yet perfected in the time of
S. Clare by reaſon of the cruell warres ouer all
Italie but eſpecially in the valley of Spoletum
ſubiect to the Church, by *Fredericke* the ſecond
ſworne enemy therof. The year 1260. the
building of *S. Georges* being finiſhed at the Popes coſt fitt to lodge therin the Religious woemen, & the owtward part to repoſe the holy
bodye of this diuine Damoſell, Pope Alexander the fourth commanded the Biſhops of
Peruſia Spoletum and *Aſſiſium* to tranſport the
holy bodye from the Church of *S. Damian* to
the new one founded to her honour which
was performed the third of October in the
preſence of a number of Prelates Abbatts and
Religious men, and great ſtore of ſecular who
reſorted from all parts in great concourſe led
by extreame deuotion, they were ready to ſtifle
each other being neuer ſatiated with kiſſeing &
embraceing theſe Odoriferous Reliques. The
Religious daughters of *S. Clare* leaueing the
monaſterie of *S. Damian* followed their mother to liue in the new monaſtery of *S. George*,
carrying with them the Crucifix which ſpake
to *S. Francis* in the begining of his conuerſion,

with

with many other holy Bodyes and Relickes; the litle Conuent of *saint Damians* doth at this present belong to the Fathers of S. *Francis* of the Reformation. Note good reader that ther is great likelhood according to our authour oft specifyed, that this sacred depositum hath bin Seuerall times transported, first from S. *Damians* to S. *George* in the City of A*ss*i*s*ium after the solemne Funeralls celebrated in presence of his Holines and his whole Court. Two yeares after from S. *Georges* againe to S. *Damian* whiles a more magnificent Church was a building it being needful to demolish the precedent. Finally fiue yeares after that to the new and magnificent Chhurch built to the honour of this glorious Ladye. The yeare 1265. Pope Clement the fifth exceedingly deuoted to the Order of S. *Clare* came expressely to A*ss*i*s*ium to visit her Church: he caused it to be blessed within and without by Cardinall *Rudulphus* Bishop of *Alba*, and he himself consecrated the high Allter, vnder which reposed the body of S. *Clare*, and Cardinall Steephen consecrated the allter dedicated to the honour of the holy saints *George*, *Cosme*, and *Damian*, with great solemnity and concourse of People, vpon Sunday the first of September.

Mirabilis Deus in Sanctis suis. Psalm. 67.

Bulle of the Canonization of S. Clare.

CHAP. LI.

ALexander Bishop seruant of the seruants of God to our venerable Brethren the Arch-bishops Bishops &c. Health and Apostolicall benediction : It being manifest that noble and renowned S. *Clare* doth shine both in heauen and in earth by the meanes of her glorious merits, with great honour and store of miracles by her perfect life in Religion and the supereminence of the eternall recompences, and doth shine heer on earth discouering vertue most cleerly by sundry signes, and because whiles liueing in this world was giué vnto her the title and priuiledge of holy Pouerty, and is repayed her in heauen with incomparable treasure, and on earth with honour reuerence and deuotion of all Catholicke Christiã people: this Virgin *Clare* by her bright workes is become resplendent and with fullnes of diuine light is most illustrious among Christians. O sacred Virgin adorned with so many titles of brightnes and light! before her Conuersion bright, in her conuersion

most

moſt bright, in Religion much more bright, &
after the courſe of this preſent life moſt reful
gent bright. This Virgin was a bright mirour
of all virtue, and from the ſweet Lilly of her
virginall purity is diffuſed a moſt odoriferous
ſent in Heauen, being vpon earth a powerfull
aſſiſtant of the needy. O admirable *Clare* who
the more wee contemplate thee in all theſe
things the more wee find thee admirable and
reſplendent in euery one, in the world cleer
and bright, in the Cloiſter a cleer Lampe, in
the houſe a bright beame, in Religion moſt reſplendent, in her life a glittering ſtarre, in her
death a moſt refulgent Sunne; giueing light
vpon earth and ſhineing in heauen. O how
great is the force of her light, and how ſparck-
ling and glittering her ſplendour. This light
was hidden and ſhutt vp in the Cloiſter of
Religion and ſhined forth , retired into a
ſtraight monaſtery, and knowne ouer all the v
niuers: ſhe was ſhutt vp in ſecret, but her
bright life did publiſh her, ſhe was ſilent and
her renowne did ſpeake, ſhe was hidden in her
Cell and knowne throughout Citties , wee
need not meruaile and wonder at this for a
torch ſo great and bright could not be without
ſplendour and light in the houſe of our Lord:
this veſſell repleniſhed with aromaticall per-
fumes could not be ſo cloſe ſhutt vp but it
would inbaulme and diffuſe an odoriferous ſet
through the whole houſe of God: and although
in the ſtraight ſolitude of her Cloiſter ſhe did

bruſe

bruse and breake the Alabaster of her body :ne
uertheles she did diffuse ouer al the Palace of
the Catholicke Church an Odour of sanctity:
being yet a young damoselle in the world she
laboured in her tender yeares to dispise and contemne vanities, and preserue the treasure of her
virginity, exerciseing her selfe in such sort in
the workes of piety and the loue of God that
from her proceeded a gratfull renowne accompanyed with excellet prayses. This being come
to the eares of S. *Francis* he began to instruct
her & aduance her in perfection & the seruice
of God, and harkening attentiuely to the doctrine of the saint, desiring to renownce the
world and the pompes therof and to follow
Christ Iesus in voluntary pouerty immediatly
effecting the intense feruour of her desires and
that she might be more perfect she distributed
to the poore and needy all her riches, in this
manner makeing her flight from the world &
going to a Church in the fieldes, her haire was
cutt of by S. *Francis* she was consecrated to
God, and placed in an other Church from
whence her kindred laboured much to withdraw her, but she cleaued so fast to the Alltar
that she drew after her the ornaments therof,
and shewing to her kindred her haire cutt of,
she resolutly resisted them saying that hauing
dedicated her heart to the seruice of God her
soule could not be separated from him, in fine
she was led by the holy Father to the Church
of S. *Damian* forth of the City of *Assisium* wher-

of she was natiue, where our Lord adioyned
to her some companions, to the end they might
coniointly liue in the continuall prayses of
their heauenly spouse *Christ Iesus*. From this
Virgin had her beginning the sacred Order of
the poore *Clares* now spread ouer all the world
this Espouse of *Christ Iesus* by the counseile of
saint Francis gaue a begining to this new obseruance; she was the first stone and foundatió
of this great Religion, being by race noble, but
far more noble and generous by her conuersió
allwayes conseruing her virginity to God as she
had dedicated it to him; after this her mother *Hortulana* considering the singular works
of her daughter entred into the same Religió
and as a good gardiner (who in the garden of
our Lord had grafted such a plant) she finished
happely her life, the Virgin *Clare* after much
importunity and to obey *Saint Francis* accepted the gouernment of her monastery and was
made Abbesse: she was the high tree seene fró
a farre couered with long boughs, bearing to
the Church the sauourous fruits of Religion:
she was the tree full of so many delightswhich
inuited and doth inuite so many damsells to
runne and tast the fruit therof vnder the sweetnes of her shade; this was the new and most
cleare Valley of *Spoleta* which giueth to drinke
of the new fountaine of liuing waters to re-
fresh and profit soules she is the fountaine deuided into many streames watering our holy
mother the Church and produceing sundry

plants of Religion; she was the high Candlesticke of sanctity so bright and cleer in the house of God that to her brightnes haue runne and doe runne many to light their Lampes at her light: It was she who in the feild of the Catholicke Faith hath planted the noble and moſt high Vine of pouerty from whence are gathered the rich fruits of ſaluation in great abundáce: it is she who in the meddow of the Church hath planted the garden inuironed with the hedges of humility, and beſett with all rigour and aſperity wherin is found plenty of all virtue she is the abridgment of the Cloiſter who with an artificiall art doth build the high and narrow tower of abſtinence wherin is prepared the ſpirituall viand of pleaſant and delectable refection: she is the Princeſſe of the poore, the Ducheſſe of the humble, miſtreſſe of the continent, and mother of the penitent: this holy virgin gouuerned her monaſtery, and Familie with much prudence in the feare and ſeruice of God, and in the perfect obſeruance of the Order, prouident in her thoughts, common in all ſeruice and labour, in counſeile moſt prudent, in admonition diligent, in correction temperate; in commaũding moderate, to compaſſion very ſenſible, diſcret in ſilence graue & in aduiſed ſpeech, very wiſe and circũſpect in all things appertaining to gouuerment: rather deſiring to ſerue thẽ to be ſerued, to honour others thẽ to be honored in ſuch ſort that her life was to others an inſtruction: learning on the booke of her life the Rule and ſquare of their

life, obſeruing as in a bright looking glaſſe
their actions and workes. This holy virgin li
ued with her bodye vpon earth, but her ſoule
was conuerſant in heauē: O veſſell of humility,
O pledge of chaſtity, O flame of charity, O
ſweetnes of benignity: fortreſſe of patience
band of peace, cōmon to all, ſweet in wordes,
meeke in workes, and beloued and ſought
of euery one. And the more to macerate the
fleſh her enemye, and fortify her ſpirit ſhe re-
ſted on the bare ground: her bed being oft
times the cuttings of Vines haueing a blocke
of wood for her pillow, her garment was one
habbitt & one cloake of groſſe and vile cloath,
contenting her ſelfe to couuer her tender bodye with this attire, ſhe wore a rude haire
cloath and Cilice wouen of horſe-haire, in eating and drinking ſhe was ſo abſtinent as a long
time ſhe was obſerued not to eat any thing 3.
dayes in the week: to wit mundayes wen
ſedays and Frydayes, the other dayes ſhe tooke
ſmall refection, ſo as the Religious were amazed how ſhe mantained life: ſhe employed the
greateſt part of her time in watching & prayer:
being allmoſt continnally ſicke being not able
to riſe to labour according to her deſire and
cuſtome, ſhe aroſe by the help of her Siſters
and being ſtayed vp by them, ſhe performed
ſome handy worke to exclude Idlenes. Her
worke was to make corporalls for the ſeruice
of the Allter ſending them in preſents to the
poore Churches and congregations about a

sisium: she was peculiarly inamoured and a curious obseruer of pouerty, it being so deeply ingrauen in her hart as dayly she became more resolute and inflamed towardes it: so strictly embraceing it as no necessity or want whatsoeuer could euer separate her from it: and would neuer consent by any counsell or aduise that her monastery should enioye any thing proper, allthough Pope Gregory the Ninth our predecessour of happy memory would haue giuen her possessions for her selfe and her Religious. Now for that such a bright light could not be hid with out spreading forth the Rayes of her beauty; she was illustrious for for many miracles: she restored voyce to a Religious of her monastery who could not be heard speake: and hearing to one that was deafe, she cured the impediment of the toung: one of a dropsie, a Freer Minor of a Frenzie diuers others makeing vpon them the signe of the crosse. An other time Oyle being wanting to the monastery she called the Brother whose office it was to begg and gaue him a vessell which the Religious Brother by the diuine goodnes and mercy fouud full. An other day it happened that the Religious woemen had in all the howse but one halfe loafe, glorious S. *Clare* commaunded the Sisters to diuide that litle bread amongst them, and in the handes of the Dispencier who distributed it, he who is the liueing bread & in the desert fed the hungrie multiplyed in such sort this loafe that haueing made 50.portions according to the number of Religious they were all sufficiently satiated and refected; by meanes of these signes and many other miracles wrought in her life was manifested the preeminencie of her merits. Now the virgin drawing neer to the end of her life she was visited with a resplendent company of virgins amongst whom there was one more glittering and refulgent then all the rest who drawing neer to the bed of the seruant of *Iesus Christ* embraced her tenderly and left her full of comfort. After her death one detained with the falling sicknes and lame of one legg being not able to goe was brought to her sepulcher and there reposeing a litle, the legg offended was heard to make a great noise as if a dry staffe had bin broken: presently he was sett free of his twoe malladies. Other Criples and diseased were cured, one who had bin many yeares blind was led to her sepulcher but returned without guide hauing recouered his sight, by reason of these workes and many other glorious miracles this venerable *Clare* doth shine so bright that in her is accomplished what her mother heard in prayer before her birth: that she should bring forth a light which should illuminate all the world, the holy Church may iustly reioyce to haue produced and nourished such a daughter who is a fruitfull mother of virtue hath by her perfect doctrine nourished and nursed vp many disciples in Religion led by her example to

the

the feruice of *Chriſt Ieſus*; the congregation of
the faithfull ought allſo to reioyce, for that
the heauenly Spouſe Ioth receaue their Siſter
for his Eſpouſe and hath placed her in the mid-
deſt of the delights of heauen: the quiers of
Ahgells and of ſaints doe ſolemniſe this feaſti-
uity in heauen with great iubilie for the new
wedding and Royall Eſpouſalls of our Lord.
It is therfore iuſt and conuenient that the Catholicke Church doe honour vpon earth her
whom God hath exalted to heauen. For this
cauſe wee with the generall conſent of all the
Cardinalls our Brethren & of all the Prelates
who are at this preſent in the Apoſtolicall
court of the Roman Church, and with their
counſeile wee confiding in the diuine power &
with the authority of his B. Apoſtles Peeter &
Paule and with our owne allſo wee doe inre-
giſter and inrole B, *Clare* in to the Cata'ogue
of holy virgins, and wee doe admoniſh and ex-
hort you by our Apoſtolicall authority commaunding you that the weluth day of Auguſt
you doe deuoutly celebrate the feaſt of this
glorious virgin and doe cauſe it with great reuerence to be celebrated by your ſubiects to
the end you may merit to haue her a fauorable
dilligent and deuout interceſſour to God for
you: & to the end that the deuotion of faithfull
Chriſtians may be the more excited and awa-
ked towardes her, and to the celebration of
her feſtiuiry, and to honour and viſitt her ſepulcher. wee confideing on the mercy of all

mighty God and the authority of the B. Apostles *Peeter* and *Paule* doe graunt vnto all faithfull Christians truely contrite and confessed
that euery yeare on her feast and the Octaues
therof visiting her sepulcher a yeare and forty
dayes pardon of the pennance inioyned them.
Giuen in the City of *Anagnie* the 18. of October 1255. and the first of our Popedome.

Notwithstanding this sacred virgin had bin
most magnificently translated, and Canonised
with the generall applause of all mē, yet there
wanted not those who detracted her gloriously triumphing in heauen, and most rashly a-
uouched she was not arriued thither, and more audaciously affirmed the Pope to be deluded
in Canoniseing of her; this rumour no sooner
came vnto the eares of his holynes but he presently wrote vnto the Superiour of the detra-
ctour, that he should first compell him to a re-
cantation and then send him vnder safe conduct
vnto his presence, the coppy of the Popes letter
as followeth.

Allexander Bishop, seruant of the seruants
of God to the Prouinciall Priour of the *Freer
Preachers* in *Germanie*, Wee are mooued with
extreame greife when wee behold those Fryers
(who haue tyed themselues to the perpetuall
seruice of God for the gaining of heauenly glory vnder a Religious habit) to be stayned with
any enormous crime, truly admireing wee haue
heard, and greeued wee declare, that a certaine
Brother of thy Order propoūding the word of

God

God at *Vienna* in Allmaigne to the people, breaking forth in to prophane wordes againſt S. *Clare*, hath preſumed with polluted lippes to reuile her, after it hath pleaſed the diuine mercy for the excellenty of her merits to illuſtrate her with admirable miracles, and the Apoſtolicall Sea with ſolemne deliberation had inroled her in the Catalogue of ſaints, affirmeing that the ſayd S. *Clare* (whoſe B. ſoule doth ſhine in the preſence of God) was not of the number of the bleſſed, & that the iudgment of the Sea Apoſtolicke in the ſayd adſcription did appeare erronious; Wherfore the temerity & raſhnes of that Brother ought to be puniſhed that with an humble hart be may deplore the exorbitance of his preſumption, and that the like boldnes be hindered in others, wee commaund vnto thy diſcretion by theſe Apoſtolicall writings in virtue of holy obedience, ſtrictly commaunding that thou inquire diligently of the truth heerof, and if thou ſhalt find it to be as is related of the ſayd Brother, that thou compell him to recant & abiure the ſayd blaſphemies in a publicke ſermon without any difficulty or dilation, premiſeing and admonition by Eccleſiaſticall cenſure, and without appellation you cauſe him by this our authority to be ſtrictly commaunded that within a competent time which you ſhall prefix him to apppeer perſonally before vs that he may receaue puniſhmēt according to his demerits, and faile not by your letters faithfully to de-

clare vnto vs whatsoeuer you shall doe heerin,
not omitting the day of his citation, nor the
forme and manner of your proceeding. Giuen
the third of the nones of Iune and the sixt yeare of our Popedome.

Of the miracles wrought by the merits of ſainte Clare, *and firſt, of poſſeſſed perſons.*

CHAP. LI.

THe operatió of miracles is a great thing
according to the Angelicall Doctour
ſurpaſſing the Order of created nature,
and in ſuch ſort appertaineth to the almighty
powerfull hand of God only, who notwith
ſtanding by his communicatiue goodnes doth
raiſe and exalt creatures to the produceing of
of ſuch effects, reſerueing neuertheles to him
ſelfe the choiſe of the creature, and the time,
and oecaſions conuenient for the doeing of
them; in ſuch ſort that this virtue can notre
ceaue her Origine from the merits of him who
worketh them, but rather from the inſcrutable
ſecrets of God, diſtributing his fauours and
benefits to whome he beſt pleaſeth and as he
thinketh fitt, for to ſay that he hath regard to
the

the sanctity of life of him by whome he will
worke such effects, it were to derogate from
the glory of many great saints ariued to the
culme of perfection and height of meritt of
whom wee read no miracles; S. *Iohn Baptist* the
Procurfour of the sonne of God, so renowned
by the testimonie of the infallible truth hath
wrought no miracles in his life, and neuertheles those who haue wrought many are not e-
steemed more holy then he; contrary wife
wee know that at the last day many shall say
Lord, Lord haue not wee prophesied in your
name, and in virtue therof cast out diuells and
wrought many miracles: and for all this our
Lord will not acknowledge them: no otherwife then the accursed traitor *Iudas* (with many others) who in company of the Apostles
did worke many miracles: S. *Hierome* vpon this
paffage faith that to prophesie, worke miracle,
and cast out diuells are not workes that doe
aliwayes proceed from the merit of him who
worketh them but rather from the inuocation
of the name of God in virtue wherof they are
done, either for the greater condemnation of
those who vse therin his diuine power leading
a life opofitt to his diuine will: or to the vtili-
ty of those who fee and hear such wonders
from whence they draw matter to prayfe and
magnify him in whofe name they are wrought
wherby wee euidently fee that such extraordinary miracles are not allwayes affured testimo-
nies of sanctity, & that God doth not comuni-

cate

cate them to all saints indifferently, but only
to those by whome he desireth to be so honored and serued as wee may obserue in his most
humble seruant S. *Clare* whom he hath made
most resplendent bright not only by the emi-
nencie of her life but allso by the splendour of
many miracles: for the satisfaction of the reader, I will make a collection of some, passing
ouer an infinite number with silence. behold
at the first incounter I presnt you with a famous victory gained by her intercessiō against
the diuell our mortall enemy, he tormented
in a strange manner a child of Perusia called
Iames, casting him one while in the fire one
while in the riuer, other whiles dashing him
furiously against the ground biteing the stones
in such rage as brake his teeth therwith, tea-
ring his haire and forceing bloud from his
head, wresting his mouth so as he seemed a
monster, so doubling and foulding his members that his feet would lye vpon his necke
he was ordinarily afflicted with these torments, in such sort as twoe men sufficed not
to guard him continually and detaine him
from acts more impertinent and outragious
as to teare his cloathes striping him selfe
naked, and kill him selfe: many remeadies
were applyed vnto him but all in vaine; his
Father named *Guidalote* dispaired euer to see
any amendment in him but in fine the diuine
clemency excited in his heart a great confidence to haue recourse vnto *sainte Clare*, who

very

very often had fubdued and tryumphed ouer
the infernall Dragon; conuerting vnto her
with moſt inward groanes he ſayd; O moſt
ſacred virgin worthy that all the world
ſhould honour thee, to thee I dedicate my
ſonne, and befeech thee to vouchſafe to reſtore him to his perfect health; and then replenished with noleſſe pyetie then confidence he led him to the fepulcher of the ſainte,
and laying him vpon it; he began prefently
to pereeaue his perfect recouuery in ſuch ſort
that neuer after he felt any ſuch mallady or
perturbation. *Alexandrina* of the towne of
Frata neer *Peruſia* noleſſe affaulted then the
precedent by an abbominable Diuell in to
whoſe power ſhe was ſo abandoned, that
he made her to Fly like a bird to the top of
the rocke neer to the riuer of Tibur, from
thence to hop to a litle branch of a tree which
hung ouer the ſayd riuer, and there hanging
to play her Idle prankes, moreouer her left
ſide was vtterly benumed and lame, the Phi-
ſitions had applyed all poſſible remeadies but
in vaine: which cauſed her to thinke vpon ſu-
pernaturall help, and excited by the great renowne of the merits of *S. Clare* ſhe went vnto
her tombe with intire confidence, and in an
inſtant ſhe was wholy freed from the oppreſ-
ſion and ſeruitude of the Diuell, and her la-
menes allſo. An other in like ſort of the ſame
place who was fallen vnder the tirannie of
the mallignant ennemye experienced the mi-

serie which followeth the the lodgeing of such abbominable ghestes: for being assaulted with many strange infirmities, in fine she cast her selfe in to the armes of the pittifull mother S. *Clare* who failed not to afford her succour and remedie and that so soone as she had recourse to her sepulcher.

Of many miraculous cures of sundrie diseases.

CHAP. LII.

A French youth goeing to Rome in company of other of his Countrymen fell sicke and lay by the way being reduced to such extreamity by the force of his infirmity that he lost his sence and became so deformed as he seemed a monster rather then a reasonable creature which much afflicted his companions, besides he became so furious that he could not be held, for the finall and souueraine remeadye they bound him vpon a Beer and earryed him to the Church of S. *Clare*, and hauing layd him before her sepulcher they all fell to prayer, and imediatly he was perfectly cured.

A Citizen of the City of *Spoletum* called

Valentine

Valentine was exceedingly afflicted with the
falling sicknes in which he fell six times a day
in whatsoeuer place he was, besides he had one
foot wholy lame he was lead vnto the sepulcher of the sainte where haueing continued the
space of twoe dayes and three nightsin great
deuotion the third day trying to stir his foot &
haueing no bodye to help him, his foot made
such a noyse by the extension and streaching
forth of the bone and sinnewes as if a peece
of timber had bin broken and incontinently
finding his legg whole he neuer felt any more
fitts of his other infirmity. A child of the same
City called Iames of the age of twelue yeares
and blind; being one day left for some space
by him that guided him, he fell in to a pitt,
brake his arme and hurt his head, the night
insuing as he slept neer to the bridge of *Verue*
there appeered vnto him a woeman who
sayd, Iames wherfore doest thou not come to
Assisium to be cured? the morning following he
arose very early and amazed at the vision he
related it to twoe other of his companyons
who were allso blind, they answered truly
wee haue heard of a Ladye who is lately dead
at *Assisium* at whose sepulcher are wrought
many notable miracles, which the young child
hearing filled with confidence hastened with
the help of his guide to to get thither, and in
his way passing by *Spoletum*, he had againe the
same vision wherfore he was more incourra-
ged and animated to prosecute his enterprise,

being come to the Church he found it so full
of People as he could gett no entrance which
much afflicted him, wherfore extreamly tired
with his iourney he layed himselfe downe in
the porch and being fallen a sleep he heard the
same voyce saying vnto him, Iames God will
be fauorable vnto thee if thou canst but gett
entrance, awakeing he beganne presently to
crye and begg of the poeple to make him
place which he obtained, but before he entred
he put of his shooes & cast of his vpper garment, and put his leather girdle about his
necke and then with great humility and reuerence he drew neer to her sepulcher and in
the interime of his prayer he fell into a sweet
slumber to whome S. *Clare* appeering sayd a-
rise Iames for thou art cured, awakeing he
found himselfe illuminated and his other hurts
healed wherfore he excited all the beholders
to sing prayses to God and his faithfull seruant
S. *Clare*.

*Of many Paralitiques and
cripples cured by
S. Clare,*

CHAP. LIII.

A Cittezen of the City of *Perusia* called
Bonne Iohn issuing one day forth of the
City with many of his fellow Cittizens
to fight against those of *Fullinium* dureing the
skirmish he receaued on his hand the blow of
a Flint stone wher-with the bone being broken he remained lame therof, he consulted
many doctours about it and applyed many rea-
medies but without any alleadgment of his
paine yea rather his dollour increased and ther
was question to cutt of his hand; but he hauing
heard wonders which God did worke by the
intercession of glorious *sainte Clare*, full of confidence he made a vowe to goe visit her sepulcher and to present vnto her a hand of wax,
being come thither with great deuotion and
leaning to her tombe dedicating him selfe to
her seruice his hand was instantly cured he
yeelding thankes to God and this blessed virgin.

A young man natiue of *Castro Bitonie* being

ſo extenuated and conſumed by a greiuous ma-
ladie which detained him the ſpace of three
yeares and reduced him to ſuch extreme weaknes as hee ſtooped allmoſt to the ground wholy deuoid of hope euer to recouuer by humaine
remeadye, for which cauſe his father who had
imployed vpon him the greateſt part of his
meanes had recourſe to the new ſainte hauing
heard the rumour of her great wonders he cauſed him to be carryed to her ſepulcher whether
he was no ſooner arriued but he began to reſ-
ſent the effect of her interceſſion, for preſently
ſtanding vp and leaping for ioye he inuited all
that were preſent to magnify our Lord and dedicate themſelues more ſeriouſly to the ſeruice of this ſainte

In the towne of S. *Quirite* within the Dioceſſe of *Aſſiſium* a child of tenne yeares old haueing bin borne pittifull lame, his feet being
wreſted awry ſo as if he were downe he could
not gett vp againe without help, his mother
had often times recommended him to S. *Francis*
but found no help, wherfore what ſhe could
not obtaine of the Father ſhe conceaued a
confidence to impetrate of the daughter for
hauing heard the admirable wonders which
were dayly related to the honour of S. *Clare*,
ſhe cauſed her ſonne to be carryed to the tombe of the ſainte; and preſently his bones were
ſettled in their due place and he was perfectly
cured.

A Cittizen of *Aguhium* named Iames of

France

France had a fonne of fiue yeares old fo lame
as he could not goe; which he took very impa
tiently it feeming vnto him that the torment
of his child was a reproch to his honour and
Familie. When this child was vpon the ground
he trailed and dragged him felfe in the durt
not hauing forces to gett vp: the Father and
mother vowed him to the fainte , promifing
that if he were cured he should be called hers;
the vowe was no fooner made but the child
was eured, wherfore not to proue vngratfull
for fo great a benefitt receaued, full of ioye
they caufed him to goe to her fepulcher.

A woeman of the Caftle Menarie called
Plenaria being long afflicted with a great paine
in her backe which fo extenuated her forces
that she could hardly goe, she caufed her felfe
to be lead to the fepulcher of the fainte, and
the next day returned without any impediment

A woeman of *Perufia* had her necke fwollen
bigger then her head with many ring-wormes
and tettars she confiding a long time in the merits of *S. Clare* in fine receaued the recompence
of her pious importunity for being one day at
her fepulcher furprifed by the night she fell in
to a great fweat wherby the humours were e
uaporated and the fwelling was alltogether
affwaged no fcarre or marke remaining.

How

How two children were saued and
rescued from the furie of the
wolues by the merits of
sainte Clare.

CHAP. LIV.

THe valley of *Spoletum* was in times past
much hanted by store of wolues which
did often prey. vpon mans flesh, ther li
ued there abouts a woeman named *Bonne* of
Mont - Gallien of the Dioceſſe of *Aſsiſium* she
had two children: one of them had bin ſome
while before deuoured by thoſe furious bea
ſtes; and the other being gone but a little forth
of the houſe while his mother was buſied in
domeſticall affaires he was caught by a wolfe
and carryed in to the woods: a labourer hauing
heard the plaintiue voice of the child knew it,
and gaue warning to the mother to looke at
home for her child, whom not finding he was
certaine it was her sonne, which plunged her
in to extreame ſorrow and impatiently bewayling she had recourſe to S. *Clare* in theſe ear-
mes ſacred and glorious Virgin *Clare* reſtore
me my child, reſtore to the vnfortunate mother her ſonne, which if you doe not I will
drowne my ſelfe: the meane while the neigh-

bours

bonrs purfued the wolfe, and found it had a bandonned the child and the doggs were licking the woundes, which the mother hearing she refumed fpirit, and with ioye she caufed him to be carryed to the tombe of the faint; yeelding thankes for the fauour receaued and acknowledged her for her fingular benefactour.

A little girle of the towne of Canary fitting at mid day in the Fields, and a woeman refting her head in her lapp ther ariued a wolfe which frighted her not for that she thought it to be a dogg: the wolfe leaping vpon her caug't her by the head and carryed her away, the woeman amazed inucked *S. Clare* faying *S. Clare* help, help, I recommend vnto you this girle. The girle yet in the teeth of the deuourer directed her fpeech to the wolfe faying, curfed theefe how dareft thou to carry any further her who is recommended to fuch a virgin? The wolfe as it were quite confounded at thefe wordes with great dexterity layd the girle downe vpon the ground and flincke away like a theefe, and the girle efcaped without hurt.

How *many were deliuered from hip wrack by the inuocation of* S. Clare.

CHAP. LV.

HE who commaundeth the windes and the *Sea* would that they should allo obay at the very inuocation of the name of this glorious fainte; for ther being gone forth of the Port of Pisa a shipp fraught with many persons, with intent to sayle towardes the Ile of Gardiana; they were no sooner entred the maine sea but a horrible tempest arose by the force wherof the bottome of the shipp leaked threatning eminent perrill and ship-wracke: these vnfortunate had recourse to S. *Clare*, makeing a vowe vnto her that if they were deliuered by her intercession they would goe all naked to their very shirts with their girdles about their neck to visit her sacred Relikes at *Assisium*, each of them presenting a wax light of two pound waight. This vow being made, they saw to discend from heauen three great lights: the one settled vpon the for-part of the ship, an other vpon the poupe, and the third vpon the pumpe, by virtue wherof the leakes where the water did enter was closed and the *Sea* became quiet and calme, and with a gratious gale of wind the vessell was accompanyed and safely conducted by the help of these three lights to the port of Aresten wherin to being entred and safely landed and all the marchandize vnfraught the lights did presently disappeer and the vessell sunke downe and was drowned, those that were gott out acknowledging the miracle deuoutly performed their vow, yealding infinit thankes to God and to the sacred Virgin S. *Clare* for the great benefit receaued by her intercession.

LAVS DEO, MARIÆ, FRAN
CISCO, ET CLARÆ.

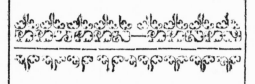

THE TABLE

OF THE CHAPTER.

how

A Table

A Table

A Table.

of

A Table

Of

A Table

APPROBATIO.

HÆc hiftoria de *vita S Claræ* ex Gallico fermo ne in Anglicum transfufa, d: gna eft quæ præli beneficie lucem accipiat, vtpote nihil habens Catholicæ Fidei ad- uerfam autbonis moribus, fed multa ad ædificationem le- gentium, Datum Duaci 24. Maij, 1635.

Georgius Coluenerius S. Theol. Do &t. & regius ordinariufque Profeffor, Colleg. ecclefiẹ S. Petri Præpofitus Duacenfis Vniuerfitatis Cancella- rius, & librorum Cenfor.

Faults escaped in the Print.

PAg. 16. in a diſtinctε character, reade diſtinctε chapter. pag. 17. for particularities, reade generalities. p. 18. fieles, reade fields. p. 19. dele it. pag. 21. Al as, reade Alas. pag. 26. one the, reade one of the. pag. 27. wherein, reade hearin. p. 28. pulchra, reade pulchri. p. 29. Antaſtick, reade Antarſtick. pag. 32. ſewed, reade ſowed. ibidem, where, reade were. pag. 33. vnto reade into, p. 35. land Bromiſe, reade land of Promiſe. ibidem, bone, reade borne. pag. 51. conuincent, reade conuincing, ibidem before his reuolt, reade before his reuolte ſolaced. ib. Margaret, r. Katherine. 52. in as, reade in as much. ibidem, ingeniouſly, reade he ingenuouſly. p. 53. 3. Order reade 3. Orders. ibidem downes Scepter, reade downe Scepters. p. 54. where, reade were. p. 56. the day, reade at the day. pag 57. grace, reade graces. pag. 59. ſhouggiſh, reade ſluggiſh, pag. 60. examplary, reade exemplarily, ibidem, his paſſion, reade of his paſſion. ibidem, Sonne, reade Sunne. pag. 61. that he, reade that as he, ibidem, which reade that which. p. 63. glorie for, reade glorie of ibidem, taske, reade taxe, ibidem, neither, reade either. pag. 65 they the more, reade they may the more, ibidem, with ground, reade which ground. pag. 66. then whoſe, reade then they whoſe, ibid. wholy, reade holy. p. 67. vocatitur, reade vocabitur, ibidem Chriſt, reade Chriſt's, ibidem hauen, reade hauing, pag. 68. haue though, reade I haue thought, p. 70. heigh, reade height, p. 71. pemomſtrated, reade demonſtrated. ibid. Romana vero dicitur, reade Romanus vero dicitur. &c,